The MYSTERY FANcier

Volume 5 Number 6
November/December 1981

The MYSTERY FANcier

Volume 5, Number 6
November/December 1981

TABLE OF CONTENTS

The MYSTERY FANcier
(USPS:428-590)
is edited and published by-monthly by
Guy M. Townsend
1711 Clifty Drive
Madison, IN 47250

SUBSCRIPTION RATES: Domestic second class mail, $12.00 per year (6 is-
sues); overseas surface mail, $12.00; overseas airmail, $18.00. Overseas subscribers please pay in international money order, check drawn
on U.S. bank, or currency; no checks drawn on foreign banks, please.
Single copy price--$2.50

Second class postage paid at Madison, Indiana.

WILDSIDE PRESS

Mysteriously Speaking ...

Ah, it's my favorite time of year again--time to ask you folks to fork over the money for another year's subscription. Last year I inserted little slips into everyone's copy of volume four, number six, reminding you that it was time to renew, but I still got an indignant letter from one subscriber later in the year chastising me for not letting him know that his subscription had expired. So this time I'm eschewing little slips in favor of full-sized renewal forms, which you will find inserted loosely in the center of this issue. You will be relieved to note that the subscription rate has remained steady at $12.00 for domestic subscribers and overseas subscribers who receive their copies via surface mail. Unfortunately, skyrocketing postage costs have forced me to raise the overseas air mail rate from $15.00 to $18.00. The cost of air mailing six issues of TMF to, say, Japan is right at $10.00 now, and I just can't afford to subsidize overseas air mail subscriptions any longer.

Since I was going to have to blow the cost of printing up the renewal form anyway, I figured it was as good a place as any to try to unload some back issues of this magazine (I need to make room for some new additions to my fossil turnip collection), so, if you're not a charter subscriber to TMF and haven't yet acquired the earlier issues, here's your chance. Volume one is out of print, but volumes three, four, and five are available complete, as is volume two (except that all the remaining copies of the first number of volume two are missing covers).

I say that volume one is out of print, and it is, but one of TMF's earliest supporters has recently returned to me her copies of volume one and the unnumbered Preview Issue. Mercenary cad that I am, I've decided to sell those seven issues to the highest bidder, and I've provided a place on the renewal form for anyone who is interested to jot down his bid. (All right, Kathi, his or her bid.)

There is also a place on the renewal form for those of you who have not yet purchased a copy of the facsimile edition of *The Armchair Detective* volume one to do so. As the publisher of that magnificent edition, I am perhaps a bit prejudiced, but the quality of the printing is absolutely superb, and the book itself is handsomely bound in quality cloth. Ask anyone who already has a copy if you don't believe me. That's enough hawking of my own wares for one issue. Now let's see what

I

some other folks have to offer.

Richard Davis (Box 1327, Harlan, KY 40831) has recently pulled off a minor miracle. Amateur publications, as everyone knows, are, well, amateurish, especially when they are aborning. Many begin life as splotchy-ditto or smudgy-mimeo printed publications, slapped together with tremendous amounts of enthusiasm and virtually no polish whatever. From these humble beginnings they sometimes stagnate and die, sometimes improve gradually through the years, or sometimes improve dramatically and rapidly and are ultimately transformed from amateur into professional magazines. *The Armchair Detective* is a splendid example of this last type. It started out great and it got better, and now it's a very slick publication indeed. Too slick, some might argue. But I digress. The point I am trying to make is that amateur publications just do not start out slick and polished with volume one, number one. Or at least they didn't until Richard Davis came along.

Richard's publication is *Huntress: The Diana Rigg/Patrick Macnee Quarterly*. It is beautifully printed on slick paper, profusely illustrated with movie stills and the like, and handsomely typeset. The 8½ x 11" saddle-stapled magazine is guaranteed to earn Davis the undying, envy-generated hatred of every amateur publisher on earth. The uncertainties of amateur publishing being what they are, Davis is not taking long-term subscriptions yet, but you can obtain a copy of this unbelievable first effort by sending him $3.00 at the address above. If you have the slightest interest in the *Avengers* TV series or its stars and other associations, or if you just appreciate fine workmanship wherever you find it, you won't want to miss this one.

After a lapse of four years, Bob Briney has finally gotten out another issue of his fine *Rohmer Review*. It's number 18, and for the Sax Rohmer/Fu Manchu fans among us who don't already subscribe, it can be had for $1.50 from R.E. Briney, 4 Forest Ave., Salem, MA 01970. Also available at the same price are numbers 14, 15, 16, and 17.

Another publication which has recently made a phoenix-like reappearance is Don Miller's *Mystery Nook,* number 13 having come out this past summer. Don's subscription terms are a complete mystery to me, but I think $2.25 will get you a sample issue, together with Don's incomprehensible explanation of how subscriptions are computed. His address is 12315 Judson Road, Wheaton, MD 20906.

Two amateur publications which run to fiction also deserve mention. One, *Skullduggery,* has been around for a while but is now in new hands. It is a quarterly, and the issues are $2.50 each ($10.00 for a year's subscription). The address is P.O. Box 191, MIT Branch Station, Cambridge, MA 02139. The other is newer, with only three issues out so far. *Black Cat Mystery Magazine* is bi-monthly. A year's subscription is $8.00 and single copies are $1.75. The address is March Chase Publishing, 45 Southport St., Suite 712, Toronto, Ontario, Canada M6S 3N5. Both publish fiction by beginning writers, as well as by some who are already established.

All of this brings to mind the pressing need for an update of THE LINE-UP. How about it, Walter?

I should also mention that Enola Stewart has done it again with another of her outstanding catalogues. Number 26 is out now, and if you don't already have it, send $5.00 immediately

(Continued on page 32)

OLD-TIME RADIO LIVES
It Isn't Easy Listening to You, Blackie!

By Carl Larsen

Boston, home of the bean and the scrod, site of Fenway
Park and the Atheneum, was also *fons et origo* of one of fiction's most durable crime-solvers, Boston Blackie. This very
improper Bostonian, who seems to have avoided the burden of a
family name, came to life before Sam Spade, the Continental
Op, or even Race Williams. His immediate literary ancestor
might be considered O. Henry's Jimmy Valentine, the reformed
safecracker. Except that the Boston Blackie first encountered
in the pages of *The American Magazine* in July 1914 was anything but reformed. Over the years the character underwent a
gradual change from criminal to private detective. Radio lis-
teners who heard him order Inspector Faraday around could have
been forgiven for thinking that Blackie was the police commis-
sioner.

Jack Boyle, his creator, was a convicted criminal himself,
having served several terms in various prisons. In fact, it
was from San Quentin that *The American Magazine* received the
first Boston Blackie stories, signed "6606." By 1919 he was
publishing them under his own name in *Redbook*. There were
two Boston Blackie films (in 1918 and 1919) starring Bert
Lytell. Another, in 1922 with Lionel Barrymore, had Boyle
sharing credit for the screenplay. Boyle worked on other
films, including several more Boston Blackie efforts, but by
the late 1920's he seems to have died in rather obscure circumstances.

His creation continued, however, getting a voice--a very
distinctive one--from Chester Morris in two 1941 films. Morris made about a dozen more and took the property on the radio
in the summer of 1944. Richard Lane, who was Faraday in the
films, was also in the radio version. Richard Kollmar took
the radio role in 1945, continuing until the show ended in the
early 1950's. Starting in 1951, Kent Taylor played Blackie on
TV in fifty-eight episodes. Video cassettes of this show are
available, as are audio tapes of many of the Kollmar radio
shows. The one Boston Blackie book has recently been reissued
by Gregg Press, greatly embellished by Edward D. Hoch's
scholarly introduction (from which most of this biographical
information was garnered). Such a resurrection spurs nostalgia completists to hope for the sight of such as the Lone Wolf,
the Falcon, and even Mr. Keen (!) back in print.

For those who attained the age of reason around the end of
World War II, the definitive Boston Blackie will always be
radio's Dick Kollmar. Blessed with a rich baritone voice, a
"good" New York accent, and enough acting ability to overcome
the handicap of some rather limp, often horrendous scripts,
Kollmar owned Boston Blackie as much as Brace Beemer did the
Lone Ranger. It was unfortunate that TV came into the picture
when both were no longer youthful enough to be fully believable in action roles.

Kollmar, who figures as one of the many villains in a recent trashy biography of his more famous wife, Dorothy Kil-
gallen, starred with her in a radio breakfast treat, *Breakfast*

with Dorothy and Dick. The New York morning air was filled
with chit-chat about parties, their children, their canary,
midnight ice-box raids, and other problems endemic to life in
a sixteen-room Manhattan apartment. For a young listener to
hear this domestic trivia from Boston Blackie (when he should
have been out solving crimes) was to realize that things are
not always as they seem to be, nor as you would like them to
be.

Like so many other vintage radio shows, *Boston Blackie* had
an organ lead-in. Not a theme, just an abrupt burst followed
by a brief action interlude, frequently involving the criminals, which foreshadowed the plot direction. A commercial
break (in my era, R and H Beer, brewed on Staten Island) led
to the famous characterization: "Boston Blackie--enemy to
those who make him an enemy, friend to those who have no
friend."

One show, fairly typical, begins with Uncle William lec-
turing his late brother's children in the mode made famous by
Dickens' Ebenezer Scrooge. He also gently reminds Aunt Carrie
the housekeeper that she hasn't got a day's work left in her.

After the commercial message, Uncle Bill, a.k.a. William
Larson, is out in the country, calling on two extortionists.
To his credit, he stands up to Harry and Jim in the same style
he has shown to those nearer and dearer to him. He won't pay
another cent. Taking the attitude that they are only salesmen,
one of the extortionists puts a sample rifle bullet through
some crockery. Larson is adamant: he won't pay a dime. A
police siren breaks up this confrontation, but the extortionists want a business meeting later to prove that they mean
business.

Larson, convinced by the rifle, picks up the phone:
"Ring, ring."
"Hello."
"Hello, is this Boston Blackie?"
"Wait a minute, there's a mirror right here--I'll take a
look. Yes, I'm Blackie! Who's this?"
Larson offers to pay well for Blackie's trouble, to which
Blackie rejoins, "You mean you'll pay me well to get you out
of yours, don't you. What kind of help do you need, Larson?
From what I hear about you, you're the nicest guy in town."
(Some things never change.)

But before Blackie can get over to Cedar Lane, Harry and
Jim arrive. The prospective victim is facing them as they
peer into his window. It's an easy, thirty-foot shot from
which Larson is never gonna wake up. When Blackie does arrive,
humming merrily, Inspector Faraday greets him warmly: "Oh, no,
not you, Blackie. Not you again." And, a minute after stat-
ing that there are three suspects (the niece, the nephew, and
the housekeeper), the inspector opines that none of them did
it.

The niece's screams bring them running. She's under attack from her brother. Blackie lays him out, sneering, "You
fall awfully easy, Larson." (Some things never change.) "But
you're not hurt. Get up!" The niece is gratified: "I wish
you'd kill him." Their mutual accusations cause Blackie to
reflect: "Everybody disliked Bill Larson. Apparently he wound
up behind the hate ball."

The organ segues to our two salesmen. In a domestic scene,
Harry is reading the paper to Jim. This, an elegant variation

on the dumb-sidekick or faithful-animal-friend device, was another favorite method of alerting the radio audience to plot
turns. According to what Harry reads, Roger Larson is being
held for the murder of his uncle (who had not even finished
his coffee before two bullets smashed into his head). Roger
claims, however, to know who really killed his uncle. Our two
crack salesmen provide Roger with an alibi via an anonymous
phone call to Boston Blackie. Faraday does indeed let Roger
go, chiefly for lack of evidence.

Actually, Roger is ignorant of the murderer's identity.
As he and Blackie leave the police station, a black car races
by and a tommy gun opens up. They duck. The organ intervenes,
and after a commercial we pick up the story to learn that,
while Larson's arm is wounded, Blackie is fine. "Too bad,"
commiserates the gruff inspector.

However, the tommy gun has activated Blackie's gray cells;
he has a plan: the newspapers will headline that *he* knows the
killers' identities. This will bring "the killers into the
open, so we can close this case."

Meanwhile, back at the Larson manse, Aunt Carrie maintains
that she may be old, but she's still sharp enough to be aware
that Jane and Roger were being tormented by their uncle to the
point where they almost hated each other. She avers that *she*
knows who did Uncle Will in.

Inspector Faraday has joined Blackie as a "walking bull's-
eye," and he is bored with pacing up and down waiting for an
attack. "Patience, patience," enjoins Blackie. "We don't
even know where our next bullet is coming from." When they do
come, they come from a sub-machine gun in Jim's hands as Harry
drives past the two sitting ducks. By some miracle, the shots
miss, but the police trap doesn't. Harry dies in the ensuing
crash. Jim Lawrence is dying. "He's a killer, so what's the
difference?" asks Faraday. On his deathbed, Jim provides a
detailed account of the murder, stressing that the late Mr.
Larson looked right at them as they leaned into his window.

Blackie asks the police lab to investigate. The denoue-
ment takes place at the Larson home, where Blackie takes a
call from the lab. He was right! He then asks the three suspects to drink some of the coffee Uncle Bill was drinking when
he died. Jane is first, but Aunt Carrie nobly prevents her
from drinking by draining Jane's cup herself. She has been
fooled into thinking it was the poisoned brew she had prepared
to do Uncle Bill in. "You're a very smart man," she tells
Blackie, who modestly asserts that he was just guessing.

Later, Faraday tells Blackie that he looks like a canary
that swallowed a cat. Blackie toots his own horn a bit, which
draws from Faraday the comment that "It isn't easy listening
to you, Blackie." Blackie asserts that in any upcoming murder
cases "You can count me in." Faraday, hardly a treat for the
ears himself, rejoins that if Blackie butts in they'll count
him out.

No one can say with certainty where the private detective
story crossed over from character to charicature. Perhaps
Hammett himself did it when his Op personally cleaned up
Poisonville. Of course, no one who is a stickler about realistic presentation has ever found much satisfaction in the
private-eye tradition, least of all in its various radio in-
carnations. But by the late years of Boston Blackie, reality
was far, far astern.

A cursory review of "The Larson Extortion Case" will justify this indictment. Consider the criminals: the examples
here are especially dense. Would any real extortionists kill
off their only victim? Would they be lured so easily, twice,
by planted newspaper items? Even if they did believe their
identities known, wouldn't they go under cover rather than
make open attacks? Would a real killer be likely to miss so
often at such short range with a submachine gun? Consider the
Larson family: granted that such a miserly uncle could exist,
wouldn't any self-respecting niece or nephew get a job to
avoid such humiliation? Would any servant, no matter how
loyal, really take poison to protect her babies? Consider
the police: schooled in reality, we can (only with great re-
luctance) accept an incompetent policeman, but can we accept
one who lets a character like Blackie meddle to the incredible
extent that Faraday does? What self-respecting cop would let
a civilian set up the trap, spring Roger from the slammer,
contact the police laboratory to perform tests, and even take
the phone call with the results? Further, what police lab
needs a prod from a wise-cracking p.i. to perform a complete
autopsy? Would any police officer permit the cruel coffee
hoax? And what idiot family would even consider drinking
coffee alleged to be several years old? (Certainly not any
Olson or Larson family!)

Consider the plot--on second thought, perhaps there is no
need to continue flogging this dead horse. Alas, the episode
discussed here is not a conspicuously bad example; it is in
fact rather better than most of the ten or so I have. Perhaps
all are from a show in its decline. Whatever the case, listening to them was a series of melancholy encounters with a show
I had remembered fondly.

What was the secret of Boston Blackie's relatively long
run on radio? Primarily the irrepressible character of Blackie
himself, as ably portrayed by Dick Kollmar. Over the years
Boston Blackie had become more socially acceptable, moving
from jailbird and safecracker to crime-solver; so, too, his
popularity increased. The name "Boston Blackie," with its
suggestion of big-city dash, was derived, according to Boyle,
from its bearer's birthplace and eyes. The alliteration aids
in firmly fixing the name in the imagination. In common with
many other fictional sleuths, Blackie was tough, good with his
fists and his mouth, able to handle crooks and cops, and at
home in the big city. He was also attractive to women, especially to the long-suffering Mary Wesley. In the original
stories Mary and Blackie were man and wife, but apparently
over the years she was demoted to girl friend, thus eliminat-
ing the domesticity which for some diminishes adventure. On
the radio she had little to differentiate her from other faithful companions like Kato and Silver. Sometimes, as in the
episode treated above, Mary did not appear at all. Her role
was played by Lesley Woods and Jan Miner.

The significant relationship in the saga was that between
Faraday and Blackie. Next to the good guy versus the bad guys,
this classic pairing of gruff authority figure and smart-
mouthed young rebel was the most enduring conflict on the
program. Like Sergeant Quirt and Corporal Flagg of *What Price
Glory?* or Baby Snooks and Daddy, their verbal sparring was a
constant attraction. Although Blackie was always right, they
took turns bailing each other out of trouble. Richard Lane,
(Continued on page 9)

THE GREAT LIZZIE BORDEN T-SHIRT MEDIA EVENT
AND MYSTERY QUIZ

By Francis M. Nevins, Jr.

During the summer of 1978 the Editorial Board of the University of California/San Diego Extension Mystery Library had its last meeting, and its saddest, and its funniest. Saddest, because a few months later--after we'd published some thirteen classic crime novels in uniform hardcover format, plus the *World of Mystery Fiction* anthology and teacher's guide, plus our own anthology, *The Mystery Story*, plus the Hubin *Bibliography of Crime Fiction*--the project collapsed. Funniest, because the meetings were punctuated with scenes straight out of *Catch-22* or *M*A*S*H* or a Harry Stephen Keeler novel.

Like the Lizzie Borden T-Shirt Media Event.

Some communications wiz at Publisher's Inc, UCSD Extension's publishing arm, had decided that it would be good for business if the print and electronic media were to cover the board's work. But since a roomful of mystery nuts voting on what titles to reprint next was not the most scintillating story in the world, the wiz made up his mind--without bothering to ask the board or even to tell us until we'd all flown in to San Diego from around the country and it was too late to turn back--to stage a Media Event. The event which the wiz dreamed up was of a truly breath-stopping idiocy. The board was to be treated to a reading of Lillian de la Torre's one-act play, "Goodbye, Miss Lizzie Borden," performed in early nineteenth-century costume for the benefit of the churning cameras. Then we would be asked to reach a verdict as to whether or not *in real life* Lizzie had committed those fabled axe murders a century and a third ago.

The media swallowed the bait and came out to the campus in droves. My opinion of the sanity of print and tube journalists hasn't been the same since that day.

On the appointed morning we all trooped into the classroom where the show was to go on and took our seats at the long conference table, facing a roomful of empty student chair-desks. There to greet us was the wiz, carrying a pile of yellow Lizzie Borden Mystery Library T-shirts, which we were supposed to don so that the TV cameras would have some jazzy visuals.

You might think that 1978 was a bit late for classroom revolts, but I was part of one in San Diego that morning. To a man and woman we refused to put on those stupid T-shirts, although I had the presence of mind to squirrel away the specimen offered to me and keep it for posterity, just to prove all this really happened. On the theory that a Mystery Library Board in its own clothes would photograph better than a board that had walked out in disgust, the wiz canned the T-shirt gimmick, at least in part.

In the hour or so before the media were due to invade, we tried to conduct our regular business. Then the fun began. Small numbers of UCSD students began trickling into the room, each of them sporting, with more or less embarrassment, a yellow Lizzie Borden Mystery Library T-shirt handed out by associate wizzes along the walkways of the campus. These poor kids

of course were to act the parts of The Audience for the TV
cameras. The extent of their interest can be gauged by some
overheard snatches of their dialogue. "Oh, you had nothing
to do either, huh?" "Who are those guys, anyway?" "The Mystery Library? Any of them write Nancy Drew?"

The cameras and their human appendages started to arrive,
and when all the media were ready, the actors entered. I use
the word in a fit of charity. Actually, they were a couple of
drama students decked out for the event in El Fako nineteenth-
century costumes and armed with copies of the de la Torre play.
Throughout the reading, the actors kept their backs to us board
members for whom they were supposedly performing and their
faces in the direction of the cameras. It was an unforgettable
rendition. I remember with special fondness the young fellow
who was assigned to read the author's stage directions. "The
bell rings," he would say, and follow it up with a lusty and
loud "BRRRIIINNNGGG!!!" Every member of the Board will swear
that that one-act play seemed to go on and on for hours.

Finally that part of the ordeal was history and we were at
bat. Each of us, with the cameras grinding, was asked for his
verdict: did Lizzie ax her parents, and if not who did? One
or two of us actually took it as a serious question and tried
to give a straight-faced answer. Most had made up our minds
to treat this clown show with the dignity it deserved and
played a game among ourselves to see who could come up with
the silliest solution. When my turn came, I put on a solemn
face and announced that during the reading I'd been weighing
the evidence in my mind according to strict legal criteria.
Then I tossed a coin on camera, pronounced Lizzie innocent,
and ruled that the real axe murderer was the Least Likely
Suspect in the play--the Borden pussycat. Bob Briney, whose
turn came after mine, offered a theory even more outrageous.
By such devices we survived the Media Event, and it will surprise no cynic that we did get a chunk of air time that evening and space in the next morning's papers.

After the Board meeting UCSD had scheduled a program to
recoup expenses, a mystery fiction workshop with all of us as
guest lecturers. It was a lot of fun both for us and, I think,
for the people (many of them teachers of mystery-fiction
courses on the high-school level) who came out to the campus
to hear us. But at the workshop's end, so as to justify giving academic credit for what was basically a two-day bull
session, UCSD handed out a test. The laws of libel forbid me
to speculate on who drafted it. Its questions reminded me so
poignantly of the recent Media Event that I decided to answer
them myself. When I'd finished my answers, I liked them so
much that I decided not to turn my paper in but to preserve it
in the archives as a memento. Here, then, just as I wrote
them, are the reflections of a black-belt scholar of the genre
on the dillies propounded to me that day.

EXAMINATION QUESTIONS

1. To what do you attribute the great popularity of mystery fiction?
   A: *The fact that it is read by so many people.*

2. Mystery literature is divided into a number of sub-genres. List five.
   A: *Private eyes, private ears, vacuum cleaner salesmen detectives,*

9

Martian invader procedurals, and I forget.

3. How does today's mystery literature differ from the style used in the "golden age"?
   A: *More sex and violence. Less gold.*

4. Select any mystery author of your choice and define what it is about his or her work that most appeals to you. Or disturbs you.
   A: *This is a sexist question and I plan to sue UCSD for asking it!*

5. In what form of the mystery would you most like to write? Give reasons.
   A: *Sex and violence. Sells best.*

6. To what extent do you believe that violence belongs in mystery literature?
   A: *A character who can't be carved up with an electric knife isn't worth the effort of putting him on paper.*

7. Do you believe that sex has a proper place in mystery writing and, if so, to what degree?
   A: *Every character in a mystery should be either male or female. Or both.*

Answer any five questions, and indicate your answers by number.

Max Rafferty, where were you when you were needed?

(Continued from page 6) Maurice Tarplin, and Frank Orth played the radio Faraday.

Judging from the examples I have, the show leaned heavily on humor. That humor leaned heavily on the pun. This play on words, paronomasia as the scholars term it, is a flimsy base for an adventure show's dialogue. For many, there are more groans than grins in puns. Perhaps inevitably, it was left to Bob and Ray to do some of the best Boston Blackie humor with their "Hartford Harry, Private Eye." Still vivid in my memory is their mid-fifties TV show on which the zoot-suited Ray as Hartford Harry has his broad-brimmed hat lifted and his head dusted off before being sapped.

Where is Boston Blackie today? A fading memory like R and H Beer, the character seems to be permanently part of the past. Both actors most closely associated with the role, Chester Morris and Richard Kollmar, came to melancholy ends. Better to remember Boston Blackie and them in their prime, with a quick fist and a quicker quip. Then, too, there is always the hope that, like the city of Boston itself, our hero may enjoy a sort of urbane renewal and once again flourish as "Boston Blackie! Enemy to those who make him an enemy; friend to those who have no friends!"

A REPORT ON

THE CRIME WRITERS THIRD INTERNATIONAL CONGRESS

By Iwan Hedman

There have been three International Crime Writers Congresses. The first was in London in 1975, the second in New York in 1978, and the third was in Stockholm this June, during the so-called Middlesummer-week.

Arrangements for the Stockholm congress were made by the members of the Swedish Academy of Detection. Though we were not officially charged with the responsibility until 1978, we knew as early as 1975 that the 1981 congress would be in Sweden, so we had plenty of time to plan for it.

At the beginning, we thought that we would not be able to properly handle more than five hundred delegates, and we made our plans with that as the upper limit. We were, therefore, stunned with the response to our first mailing of information. Twelve hundred people--from Africa, Japan, New Zealand, all over Europe, and even from behind the Iron Curtain--wrote to say that they were interested in coming.

We witnessed a similarly enthusiastic response to our "World's Best Short Story" competition. We invited authors from all over the world to submit original stories, the best eighteen of which would be published in an anthology in 1982. We received over five hundred responses, some of them very curious indeed. Some were written on cloth, and some were even embroidered--and some African authors even wrote to us asking for paper to write their stories on.... First prize in the contest was a brand-new 1981 Saab Turbo; second prize was an around-the-world trip provided by SAS; and third prize was a tour of Scandinavia. (The second and third prizes were for two people and included $1,000 pocket money.)

At first we planned a very large and complicated program, but we eventually shortened it in order to leave some of the evenings free for the delegates to do other things such as go shopping and visit with friends.

For the people making the arrangements, those three years of planning seemed to fly by, but when June arrived we were ready to take care of the influx of delegates from all over the world. As it happened, only about three hundred people actually attended, so we were able to handle the congress in a proper way.

For my wife and me, the fun began earlier and lasted later than the scheduled festivities. For some days before the congress, Angus Ross, Desmond Bagley, and Desmond's wife, Joan, were guests in our home, and afterwards we had the pleasure of entertaining Walter Wager, Otto Penzler, Aaron Mark Stein, and their families.

The congress was held at the Grand Hotel, conveniently located close to everything right in the middle of Stockholm. The management of the Grand Hotel entered into the spirit of the thing by offering a free week for two in one of their deluxe suites to the author of the best novel set at least in part in the hotel itself. Entries must be submitted before 1 June 1982, and the judging will be done by a jury of members of the Swedish Academy of Detection.

The congress opened with a splendid Swedish lunch at the Stockholm City Hall on Monday, 15 June. The meal was followed by a book auction and a panel discussion of "Crime Writing in Different Countries and Cultural Environments."

The auction was in two parts. Swedish books, including many very rare and scarce items, came first, then came the English and American books. (After the auction I heard one man say, "Thank God that Otto Penzler was here from New York.") Among the choice items present were a bound copy of *Graham's Magazine* containing Edgar Allan Poe's first short stories (it sold for 11,000 Swedish kronor) and a very rare, signed, first edition of the first Murder Dossier--Dennis Wheatley's *Murder off Miami*--with the seal at the end unbroken. Later that day, delegates were invited to attend a "Criminal Exploits" exhibition at the Royal Library.

The next morning's program began with "Crime on the Stage," proceeded through "Trial," and ended with a panel on "Witness Psychology." At noon, delegates were transported to Stockholm's oldest prison, Långholmen (roughly translated, it means Long Island), and treated to a typical outdoor Swedish meal of pea soup, mustard, and beer. Unfortunately, it rained throughout the entire meal. After standing for some time, holding a plate full of pea soup and rainwater, Fred Dannay (half of Ellery Queen) turned to his wife, Rose, and said, "Let's go home." I could well understand how he felt.

After lunch we had an opportunity to go inside the prison-- which contains a special cell built at a cost of two billion Swedish kronor to house Sweden's most famous spy, Wennerström --and take a close look at this very old structure. Then, after a short sight-seeing tour of Stockholm by bus, it was back to the Grand Hotel, where the afternoon was rounded out by a lecture on "The Terms of Writers" and a very interesting Sherlock Holmes causerie by Sweden's famous Sherlockian, Ted Bergman, which included a short film of Sir Arthur Conan Doyle talking about his most famous creation.

The evening's activity, arranged by *Dagens Nyheter*, Sweden's largest morning paper, was to have been an outdoor get-together at Mosebacke Square, at which the crime writers could meet and mingle with their public. Because of the continuing rain, not many people showed up, but Ellery Queen, Hillary Waugh, Desmond Bagley, Christianna Brand, and several others gave a presentation on stage.

Wednesday morning the delegates were treated to one of the best programs of the congress when they were bused over to the Stockholm Police High School for "A Day with the Police." The program, which was greatly appreciated by the delegates, included segments on equipment, shooting, self defense, investigation techniques, and the use by police of dogs and horses. Lectures on "Forgery in Art" and "Fingerprints on Acts" and a panel discussion on "Why Do Poeple Enjòy Reading About Crime?" took up the afternoon.

That evening was *the* evening of the congress for me and my DAST, as we had planned a cocktail party at our home in Strängnäs. Since Strängnäs is about seventy kilometers from Stockholm, the 150 invited guests were transported to and from the hotel in two large buses. The weather was bad all day, and we were afraid it might rain on the party, but half an hour before the party started the sun broke through and the clouds quickly disappeared. We were told that people in one of the buses driving to Strängnäs burst into applause when the sun came out. The party was a great success, and when the buses loaded up for the trip back to Stockholm late that night, most of the people looked happy (some did not, I can't understand why ...).

Thursday morning's program was devoted entirely to a panel discussion entitled "Make Your Crime Novel a Bestseller!" The discussion was divided into two parts: "Home Market" and "International Market." For lunch, the delegates were transported to Manilla, the residence of the Bonnier Publishing Family, located in Djurgården, one of the most beautiful parts of Stockholm. After lunch, buses took us to Södra Theater, where we heard a talk on "Writing for Stage and Screen," and after that we were on our own until morning.

Friday, of course, everyone was looking forward to the Gala Dinner, but there were several other programs before then, including two panels on "Women and the Crime Story" and "Realism or Escapism in Crime Novels." Participants such as Christianna Brand, Ruth Rendell, and Michele Slung made these humorous as well as interesting.

After a free afternoon, at last it was time for the Gala Dinner. Everyone was, of course, curious about who would win the Saab Turbo for writing the best short story in the world in 1981. The winner, Frank Sisk, was virtually unknown in Sweden and the rest of Europe, though I understand he is well known in the United States. There were a lot of speeches-- some of which, as usual, were too long--and the food got cold, but otherwise it was a great evening. We had planned to have a dance after the dinner and the ceremonies, but they lasted too late and people just disappeared afterwards.

The only activity scheduled for Saturday, the last day of the congress, was a boat trip to Åland. It was a sunny day and the food was very good. Unfortunately, it was Midsummer-night there and all the shops were closed when the boat arrived. Still, everyone seemed to enjoy the trip.

Besides the regular program, a number of outside activities were scheduled to coincide with the congress. These included:

"Detectives on Stamps," an exhibition taken from my own collection;

"Sleuths of Archaeology," at the Historical Museum;

"Criminal Exploits," an exposé, at the Royal Library, of the Swedish crime novel from the end of the nine-teenth century to the present day; and

"The Swedish Crime Novel Abroad," an exhibition of translations of Swedish crime novels, arranged by the Public Library of Stockholm.

Additionally, the Police Museum was open the entire week.

I don't know how interesting and entertaining this is to read about if you weren't there, but for those of us who were right in the middle of it, trying to entertain all the world's best authors in our beloved genre, it was a tremendous event.

We don't know today where the next congress will be--or even if there will be another one--but we have heard Tokyo and Los Angeles mentioned, and if it is in either place I can only say, "See you then and there!"

A special issue of DAST--presenting about twenty of Sweden's most famous living mystery writers and their work, illustrated with jackets and photos--was published, in English, for the Congress. There are still some copies in stock, and they are for sale at $2.00 per copy. Write to Ivan at DAST, Flodins Väg 5, S-152 00 Strängnäs, SWEDEN.

DOCTOR WONDERFUL

By Bob Sampson

In the murder room, the police stand baffled, wringing
their great red hands.

Through the windows, the 1920's sun, a simpler star back
then, illuminates another scene from another mystery in another of the early pulps. There the dead man sprawls, strangely killed. There the suspects whisper. Clues sprinkle the
room--Javanese krises, demijohns of untraceable poison, cryptic notes with pieces of importance ripped off.

Who could possibly have done this dreadful thing?

How possibly can these official lunkheads detect the
guilty?

The solution, as every reader knows, is to request outside
help. And even now, help stands in the doorway.

> ... a slight, girlish figure, clad in a long gray coat. A scarlet
> tam was pulled tightly over her unruly bobbed hair.

Her face is delicate with "finely moulded features." Dark
eyes glow under delicate level brows. Her musical voice speaks
in gently pedantic diction, as if her veins were filled with
liquid synonym.

She is Dr. Nancy Dayland, Nancy Drew grown up, every girl's
dream of what she will be when she becomes a famous criminal
investigator.

> Could this slip of a girl be some noted specialist--some famous
> confrere in the medical profession?

Why sure. In the early 1920's half the practicing detectives were doctors, an unexpected consequence of Dr. Thorn-
dyke's success. Dr. Dayland, for instance, has solved twenty
major crimes in less than a year. Now, when she comes tapping
at the door, big, coarse, tough lawmen crumble and turn over
all their professional troubles to her. Before she opens her
mouth (delicate, sensitive, red), they begin sniveling with
gratitude.

> The world, in general, until lately, had been particularly chary
> and slow to accept the unusual ability of a feminine criminolo-
> gist. Yet this Chinese sluggishness of mind had monthly been
> dissipated by the girl's real achievements, her service to the
> safety of society.

That is the authentic and real opinion of Florence Mae
Pettee (1888-   ), writer of the Dayland series, gasping in
deep and profound admiration as she doubles and repeats her
words and qualifiers again and also once more.

Florence Mae Pettee and her remarkable prose appeared in
the pulp magazines during one of those periods when old practices were dying and new ones were not yet ripe. In this case,
"old practices" means certain editorial assumptions that had
served the pulps well in the years before 1920. The initial
assumption, from about 1903, was that an all-fiction magazine
should contain at least one thing to please each member of the

family--from golden-haired Nellie to Old Grandpa Pepperbox.
As a result, the prose in such representative magazines as *The Argosy*, *Popular Magazine*, and *Blue Book* vary wildly--from simple boys' action adventure to adult complexities of mysticism and ethical decision. Only gradually did the fiction magazines narrow their offerings to a less diffuse readership.*

During the mid-teens, it was discovered that women were buying a great many pulps. The immediate reaction (Assumption #2) was that sales would benefit if a woman's slant could be introduced. This resulted in an abrupt increase in the number of feminine lead characters in *The Cavalier* and *All-Story Cavalier Weekly* and culminated, around 1922, with a series of decorative girls simpering from the cover of *Argosy All-Story Weekly*.

Florence Pettee's work fit with moderate success into this climate. Her heroine, a bright young thing, seems directed toward teen-aged girls--a specific element of readership and feminine to boot. The stories themselves are inadvertent travesties on the detective story, but that is entirely another matter.

Pettee's work is scattered across the magazines of the period. Only a partial checklist is available, but her fiction has been noted in *Black Mask* (1921), *Action Stories* (1923), *Argosy All-Story* (1923), and *Flynn's* (1924). The stories are third-generation Sherlock Holmes, with a strong dose of girls' book fiction stirred in.

The earliest Dr. Nancy Dayland story reviewed is "The Scarlet Spider," from *Action Stories*, March 1923. In this, a fellow rows out alone into the bay, while three witnesses watch. Suddenly he is mysteriously dead, a heavy knife rammed through him. And there, freshly painted on the rowboat side, where nothing had been a moment before, appears what seems to be a scarlet spider and the number "13."

What can it all mean?

What invisible hand slew this man?

It takes Dr. Nancy a single day to uncover the meaning of the painted symbols (which is "July 13"). She also identifies the weapon (a bow gun that hurls knives) and the motive (revenge for "playing the cad").

All perfectly clear--if you have straight slim brows and access to the dead man's diaries.

You will be pleased to learn that the murderer never sets foot in the story.

"The Mystery of Voodoo Manor" (which even sounds like a Nancy Drew title) ran in *Argosy All-Story* as a four-part serial, July 21—August 11, 1923. Among the cast is featured:

> a creature dark like a shadow, yet so transparent that the moon shown through it, lining out, in spectral ghastliness, its bone structure beneath....

In addition to that bit part, there is a murder, a vanishing knife, a corpse rolled over in the coffin, a mysterious

---

*This point is covered in detail by Sam Moskowitz in his essay, "A History of the Munsey Magazines," which is found at the back of his anthology, *Under the Moons of Mars*. *The Fiction Factory* by Quentin Reynolds also touches on this matter.

peddler who keeps altering his disguise, and an old lady with
a pet bat. Nancy discovers the meaning of each and every one
of these wonders. Madame Pettee grows hoarse telling us how
exciting it all is.

Very soon, one serial begins to look like another.

Murder is done. Black menace looms out there, wuffing and
snorting offstage. Dark figures stalk. Weird noises chill.

For all this stage dressing, actual violence is meticulously
avoided. Nancy must be protected at all costs. She may be
baffled, but Pettee never allows her to be endangered. In
consequence, there is essentially no physical conflict and no
rough stuff at the end of a story to boost the adrenalin.

Absence of a concluding action scene leaves a distinct
hole. This is filled by the threadbare seance scene, familiar
to lovers of B movies and the adventures of Craig Kennedy,
which established this type ending back around 1912. What the
scene amounts to is that the detective calls all the suspects
together, dazzles them with dramatic pyrotechnics, and exposes
the guilty. "Thou art the man." Consternation! Amazement!
Drama after a fashion.

Dr. Dayland is partial to such endings. At the end of
each serial, she calls in all the suspects and dazzles them
with her mind. (She is above tight blouses.) Under the
prose, the breathless gigglings of a pre-teen girl is clearly
audible: See me, Daddy, how clever I have become; see how they
admire me.

Nancy explains in detail how she discovered who did it.
Then the murderer explains that he did it that way. Then all
the characters allow that they will be happy all the rest of
their lives. It's heart warming.

At these feasts of reason, very little hard evidence is
presented. Nancy is rather above evidence. She doesn't need
it, for the murderer will confess, once he has learned how
that delicate little girl with the bobbed hair has seen right
through his complicated scheme.

Sometimes he commits suicide, and that's as good as a con-
fession. Besides, with suicide you need no proof at all.

Not that proof is really needed. Dr. Dayland says it's
so, and it's so. She does not fail. The poor child is not
allowed to fail. Failure might put wrinkles on her delicate
olive-skinned face or thin those bright lips. Florence Pettee
has the very warmest regard for Nancy Dayland, famous doctor
and criminologist.

Not only is Nancy not allowed to fail, she may not even be
successfully challenged. If a maid answers her pertly during
an interview, Nancy daunts the saucy thing with the power of
her eye, leaving her trembling and subdued.

If a jealous police detective scoffs at female investi-
gators, the chief of police immediately recognizes that the
fellow is dangerously unstable.

If, during a fencing exercise, Nancy's opponent unleashes
a fancy attack, Nancy adroitly flicks the foil aside and
touches the heart.

Can't fail, can't be challenged. Has personal force,
beauty, talent, respect, admiration....

Drusilla Deming admires Nancy without reservation. Drusilla plays the part of Dr. Watson in these chronicles, being
much slower than the reader and sugar-mouthed when speaking of
the excellence that is Dr. D.

A tiny, gray-eyed girl, Drusilla is younger than Nancy, her closest friend, and is as much of a caricature. "Her mind," we are told, is as "unscientific as Nancy's was the reverse. Still, the paint-daubing art student often quite naively hit upon a question that set Nancy's train of thought in the correct direction."

For about five years, Drusilla has been prancing along in Nancy's wake, extravagantly admiring. It makes you feel a little sorry for clever Dr. Dayland. All day long she thinks in a beautifully decorated office, exquisitely feminine. Clients enter; Drusilla bounces in. But clients are business and Drusilla is a light-weight. Nowhere is there a hint of an equal.

No man engages Dr. Nancy's interest. No social life mars her magnificent isolation. Does she like music, do you suppose? Does she dance, or drive fast, shop for improbable antiques, like books or birds? Has she ever heard a jazz band? Some fine bands in town in 1923. How does she feel about jade or Scott Fitzgerald or the *Smart Set*? Has Drusilla ever mentioned Paul Klee? Do they giggle over "A Nude Descending the Staircase"? Does she like franks with chili, Florida land investments, Charlie Chaplin, Zeb Confrey?

Why does she have to sit in that tastefully appointed office and never touch the rich world that flashes and crackles just outside that window? Out there, it is the 1920's. Inside poor Nancy sits, supremely perfect, waiting for her twenty-first major case and the adulation she must have grown to resent.

A few weeks after Voodoo Manor, another case begins. This was published as "Marked Down" in *Argosy-All Story Weekly*, four parts, September 29 — October 20, 1923. Outside a medium's office in a tall building lies a man stabbed to the heart.

"I killed me," he gasps--and dies.

The police fumble. It is Nancy who discovers the diamond-set miniature concealed in a secret drawer in the decorative Chinese dragon. She alone inspects the floor where the body lay and discovers the tell-tale dent. Just as later she discovers the fragment of a will, the blotter stained with dead man's blood, the significance of a cut-out muffler on a passing automobile. It is a straight-forward mystery solved by intelligence and blame few hard facts.

At first glance, the murderer has such familiar characteristics that you blink. Here, at the climax of the story, is Dr. Dayland, telling him how he went about his fiendish deed:

Your clothes were black throughout, even to your long overcoat, your soft black hat and a wide silk muffler bunched high, covering the lower part of your face and any chance gleam of white from your shirt front. On your hands, you probably wore thin black gloves. Your hat was pulled low over your face. You were dressed like the prince of darkness, like the lurking shadow of impending evil. [*Argosy-All Story*, 20 October 1923, p. 300.]

Before this quotation creates a brand-new theory of the origin of the lead character in *The Shadow Magazine*, it might be just as well to remark that Bruce Graeme (Graham Jeffries is the real name) had published the first Blackshirt stories in the English *New Magazine* in early 1923. Blackshirt was a slick gentleman crook who wore dark clothing, his wonders to perform. His working attire closely matches Pettee's description of the "prince of darkness." The influence of Graeme is probable, although not proven.

A four-part serial, "Death Shod," ran in *Flynn's*, November 8-29, 1924. Someone bad has stabbed a young woman and hurled her over a sea cliff to the beach. The sheriff, a shrewd fellow, swiftly gets out of his depth. He engages Nancy's services. --Can't offer you much but glory, he says. But Nancy is uninterested in money:

It's the spirit of the chase--the ferreting out of the obscure that is ample reward.

You don't pay much income tax on the spirit of the chase, either.

Nancy spends most of the novel in disguise. The story is another wonderful stew--family insanity, a wealthy counterfeiter, a murder weapon concealed in a jar of strawberry preserves. And secret passages and a secret door concealed in a cliff. And suicide disguised as murder, and suicide disguised as suicide. It's every bit as interesting as Nancy Drew, and much longer, too.

In this serial, as in all the others, the prose is elliptical and full of gas. Madame Pettee is unable to approach a single word head on. Thus:

Newspaperman = *Carrions of morbidity*
Blood = *Life-Giving Fluid*
Boast = *Flagrantly and defiantly flaunt*
Killing = *The annihilation of life*
Looks like = *Typifies the picture in every essential*
Conscience will hurt = *The weight of the knowledge will become burdensome*
Thought something wrong = *Surmised that something untoward had occurred.*

Nouns are richly dressed in adjectives:

An odd lantern cast a weird light through its elaborately carved and silk-shaded sides.

And sentences are so decorated that their knees buckle:

He, too, had not yet learned the fallacy of fatuous regrets and petty jealousy.

The rolling of the boat in the angry sea will preclude the possibility of striking so tremendous and so unerring a death-wound.

That last quotation means that a man swimming beside a boat couldn't have stabbed the victim because the boat pitched so. (The problem is found in "The Scarlet Spider.") Therefore, the murderer must have stood on shore, two hundred yards away, in a cross-wind, and fired a knife with the wind profile of a billboard, into a victim seated in a rolling, yawing, pitching rowboat....

"The cryptic and the unusual," says Nancy, "always fascinate me."

Such a sweet girl. And just in her twenties.

A PARTIAL CHECKLIST OF FICTION BY FLORENCE MAE PETTEE
(Stories known to be about Dr. Nancy Dayland identified by *)

In *Black Mask*

"The Clue from the Tempest," June 1921 (novelet)

"The Double-Bottomed Casket," July 1921 (short story)

In *Action Stories*

"The Scarlet Spider,"* March 1923 (short story)

In *Argosy-All Story*

"The Mystery of Voodoo Manor,"* July 21, 28, August 4, 11, 1923 (serial)

"Marked Down,"* September 29, October 6, 13, 20, 1923 (serial)

In *Flynn's*

"Death Shod,"* November 8, 15, 22, 29, 1924 (serial)

BOOK PUBLICATIONS

White Dominoes, Whitman, Reilly, [1921].

The Palgrave Mummy, Payson & Clarke, 1929.

Blunder's Mystery Companions, 1929.

TWO FROM THE TELLY

British fan Bob Adey gives us a look at two TV series
which are unlikely to air in the United States.

SAPPHIRE AND STEEL

The first thing to comment on in this highly unusual series is its timing. It has mainly been shown at the unsual
times of 7:00 and 7:30 p.m. Tuesday and Wednesday evenings.
Each particular story lasts anything up to eight episodes with
no indication until the last week of the story that the end is
nigh. It is not surprising, therefore, that, of the five stories televised so far, I have only seen one in its entirety and
most of two of the others (one of which was made even more difficult by a television strike).

Each episode opens with a view of twinkling stars and a
deep voice announcing, "All irregularities will be handled by
the forces controlling each dimension. Transuranic elements
may not be used when there is life. Medium atomic weights are
available." He then lists the atomic weights concerned, starting with gold and ending with sapphire, silver, steel. "Sapphire and steel," the voice concludes, "have been assigned."

Sapphire is in fact tall and attractive Joanna Lumley
(Purdy of *The New Avengers*), and Steel is David McCallum.
Each of these extra-terrestrial policemen, as one character
described them in the last story, is possessed of strange powers and makes regular and necessary use of them in pursuit of
the unnamed, undescribed, unseen enemy which is ready and able
to tamper with the fabric of time to achieve its evil goal.

The series is an excellent one for twists in plot, use of
occult themes, and cliff-hanging situations. To try and give
you an idea of the flavour, I can do no better than to describe
two of the plot lines in the series (the second and fifth, as
it happens).

(1) The scene is a small, disused railway station (there
are many of them in Britain nowadays) where a male medium is
trying to make contact with the dead. There are indeed spirits abroad, but not the traditional clanking chains and regency
shapes. The ghosts are those of young men who have died in
combat in World War I and II, young men whose spirits are bitter and resentful of those they consider to have sent them to
young and undeserved deaths. And this resentment has been
harnessed by the unseen presence whom Sapphire and Steel pur-
sue. The young men have been promised, so it seems, their
reincarnation, and here is a meddling medium unaware of the
force with which he is dealing. The sets of the disused station and its musty and gas-lit rooms form a splendid backdrop
for the drama that unfolds as ghostly figures in World War I
trench uniforms or pilots' outfits materialize and vanish just
as mysteriously. Steel and Sapphire both face dreadful dan-
gers (Steel is almost trapped in a facsimile of a plummeting
aircraft), and a dreadful sacrifice has to be made before the
evil is forestalled.

(2) Lord Mulroon has organized a period party at his
country house to celebrate the summer solstice. All his guests
attend in costume suitable for the year 1930, but then the fun
really starts. Two unexpected guests arrive (Sapphire and

Steel, who else?), and then it is discovered that time really has moved back to 1930. The guests remain amazingly unperturbed, even when a further surprise guest appears who bears a remarkable resemblance to Mulroon's partner, McDee, who died in mysterious circumstances the night of the summer solstice-- guess which year?--1930!

The initial and unnatural calm of the situation (unbroken even when it is discovered that no one can leave the house) is suddenly shattered when one of the guests is brutally murdered. Sapphire and Steel, soon openly playing the role of detectives, deduce (after a second brutal killing) that someone, or more probably something, is killing the guests off in order of age-- youngest first, until everyone is eliminated who was not alive in 1930. They also deduce, quite correctly, that it really is the late McDee, and not an impersonator. It remains for them to work out why time has been turned back in this way, and, since I gather that you're not likely to find out in the States, I can reveal that the reason is a quite logical one. McDee was on the point of a great discovery when he was killed in 1930--but his discovery was a dangerous and uncontrollable microbe which would have brought about the total destruction of mankind. Thus his death (he was accidentally shot by his lover) prevented a worldwide disaster, and it was this situation that the malignant being wished to rerun and, this time, complete in the worst way possible. But Sapphire and Steel naturally save the day . . . .

I hope that this will give you some idea of this quite unique series. To be frank, the answers and the endings are sometimes unsatisfactory, and there is inevitably a lot you have to surmise. But it is good fun and chockablock with the most imaginative ideas. If you do get it in the States, watch it. You could find yourself well and truly hooked.

THE PROFESSIONALS

I've a lot less to say about this show, because it's much more of a wartime series. These are the men of CI5 (Home Affairs (S) Department), and their function is to fight violence with violence. Terrorists, hit squads, urban guerrillas: these are the people they're up against, and no quarter's given.

The team is led by Controller George Cowley, and his two main men are Bodie and Doyle. Other players feature occasionally, and often perish for their troubles, but then those are the men the series is built around.

Cowley is played by Gordon Jackson (you'll remember Hudson of *Upstairs, Downstairs*), and Bodie and Doyle are Lewis Collins and Martin Shaw, probably both unknown on American television. The three characters, as played by their actors, go a long way toward making the series the success it is. The other vital ingredient is the action scenes, as good as anything served up in the equally popular *Sweeney*. The plots? Well, good enough, but there is a sameness to them. After all, how many different ways can you knock out a terrorist group, foil an assassination, etc., etc.

If it reaches the States, I'm sure that it will have just as good a following as it has at home.

A final note. The Professionals appear in a series of about eight paperback thrillers and two large-size junior

(Continued on page 32)

ONE IN TWO

SOME PERSONALITY STUDIES BY RUTH RENDELL

By Jane S. Bakerman

Though Ruth Rendell is widely known as the creator of Inspector Reg Wexford, one of the most popular fictional detectives ever to appear in a series of novels, she is perhaps
even more important as a student and recorder of the human
personality. A significant factor in the Wexford series is
the author's careful attention to characterization. No plot
ever arises from gratuitous manipulation, but, rather, motivation always springs from well-conceived, vividly rendered
characters.

This skillful attention to characterization and motivation
is no accident, for Rendell herself has pointed out that "the
development of a human personality is what I'm really interested
in. I like to work on characters. I want to know what will
become of them. . . . I'm very interested in the pressures
that are put on people and the stresses that they suffer from
other people."* The author's central interest, the development, the integration, or the disintegration of an interesting
personality, is the driving force behind a second group of
works, novels which usually appear alternately with the Wes-
ford books.

These novels are the stories of men and women under pres-
sure, people facing major personal or professional crises.
The crises are generated or exacerbated by a crime, but the
true centers of interest are the stresses the central characters suffer at the hands of other people and the protagonists'
reactions to those stresses. These works are serious studies
of contemporary men and women, and they elevate Rendell's work
well above most crime fiction.

Among these non-series novels are two in which Rendell has
examined pairs of characters who are surprisingly alike while
also being very unlike one another. They can almost be said
to be two parts of the same personality or comparable and con-
trastable examples of how a positive character can become dangerously like his less attractive counterpart. The plots of
the novels are entirely different from one another, and the
four characters stand alone very nicely, but comparing and
contrasting them illustrate some basic truths of human nature.
In Sickness and in Health (Doubleday, 1966, British title:
Vanity Dies Hard), Rendell's third novel, an entertainment,
explores the personalities of two women. A much later book,
a serious examination of character and one of the author's
best, *A Demon in My View* (Doubleday, 1977, published in Britain
in 1976), analyzes the personalities of two men. Interesting
in their own rights, the books are fruitfully studied as a
pair, for they reflect the development of Rendell's authorial
skill.

*   *   *

---

*Quoted in Jane S. Bakerman, "Rendell Territory," *The Mystery Nook*,
no. 10 (1977), A3.

Alice Fielding is the protagonist of *In Sickness and in Health* and is one of Rendell's most interesting creations, even though the reader becomes a bit impatient with her because she is sometimes obtuse. One of the most self-doubting women ever to appear in a novel, Alice has almost no sense of her own worth, and that doubt affects every close relationship she undertakes. It also makes her extremely awkward with strangers; "Away from Stalstead and the people she had known all her life, Alice was always a little ill at ease, uncertain, shy." (p. 20) Too often, to assuage that shyness and uncertainty, wealthy Alice uses money to ease her way. "I pay grossly, disproportionately for everything, she thought. . . . I pay my way into and out of everything." (p. 124) In this thought, as usual, Alice is a little to hard on herself. Because she thinks she has little to give personally, and because she nevertheless sees herself in the role of supporter and comforter--"A tall, substantial woman with broad shoulders made to cry on"(p. 20)--Alice uses what she does have, money, to fulfill her self-imposed role.

In many ways, Alice Fielding has skipped her girlhood, behaved like a middle-aged person for years, because she feels incomplete as a woman. This attitude and her sense of worthlessness can be traced directly to an accident in her youth. She has sustained a crushed pelvis, and an overheard whisper leads her to believe she cannot conceive a child: "Those covert sentences had marked the beginning of a haunted childhood and adolescence. Age fast, she had prayed, find substitutes, find other outlets for your money and your love." (p. 46)

One of those outlets Alice has found (miraculously, it seems to her) is Andrew, her husband, and the other is Nesta Drage, a close friend. "Love had come to her late and unlooked for," (p. 31) and at first Alice glories in her marriage, finding value in herself because Andrew finds value in her: "She . . . looked the way she always did, a woman with a splendid figure--a fine woman, Andrew said--in a Macclesfield silk dress and sensible low-heeled sandals, her hair done in the way it had been since she had first put up the plaits when she was seventeen. Andrew had . . . fallen in love with her just the way she was. Why should she change?" (p. 29) But her newly found complacency dissipates all too easily when Alice begins to doubt her marriage, wondering, in fact, if her friend and her husband have not been lovers.

> Why had he married her, given up the job that was his life, changed his whole existence, unless he loved her? Because you are a rich woman, said a small cold voice, because Nesta lived in Salstead too.
>
> When they had first gone out together he hadn't known she was rich and the signs of love had shown themselves at once. You fool, snarled the canker that was growing inside her. Everything about you proclaimed it, your clothes, your rings, the photographs you showed him of Vair Place. On the second occasion they met she had spoken to him of Whittaker-Hinton [the family firm]. She could remember it all so clearly and now she thought she could remember that then, at that very moment, he had lifted his eyes from the picture, smiled, touched her hand, begun to show her the marked attention of a lover. (pp. 128-129)

Though she is dependent on the love of her husband for a

sense of self-value, Alice has acted as the supportive main-
stay for her immature, widowed friend, Nesta Drage. In a moment of true insight which she quickly represses, Alice wonders "if in a strange way Nesta had been her substitute
child," (p. 46) and realizes that pity has motivated the
early stages of their friendship; "Nesta had been lonely and
forlorn. It was because of this . . . that Alice had made a
point of cultivating her." (p. 42)

Some little while after Nesta has rather dramatically left
town, Alice discovers that her friend's new address does not
really exist. Alice's determined inquiries are consistently
frustrated, and she begins to suspect that Nesta has been murdered. Because she feels responsible for her friend (for her
child-substitute), Alice persists, despite warnings from other
acquaintances that Nesta may not want to be found and that
Alice is much better off without her. Thus, Alice becomes a
kind of amateur detective and undertakes her quest which is
really two-fold, for, reluctant as she is to do so, she finds
herself not only investigating the disappearance, but also un-
covering another side to Nesta's character, an unpleasant one.

On the surface, blond, pretty Nesta is a doll-like para-
gon, ostentatiously true to her dead husband's memory, and
Alice believes that her friend's delicate, polished appearance
reflects inner sweetness, always associating Nesta with the
florist shop she operates: "Inside the air was humid yet fresh
with scent. That particular perfume, a mixture of roses, acrid
chrysanthemums and the heavy langour of carnations brought
Nesta back to her as perhaps nothing else could. It seemed to
go naturally with the plump pretty face, the golden hair and
the commonplace prattle." (p. 17)

This passage includes two important clues to Nesta's real
personality. There is a hot-house quality about her, an arti-
ficiality, a sense of forced growth, which Alice, idealizing
all the while, takes for fragility and uniqueness. Actually,
Nesta *is* common. There are no depths of grief or thoughtful-
ness beneath her chatter as Alice so earnestly believes; in
fact, another character sums Nesta up very aptly: "A cross between a Jersey cow and a china doll, that's how she struck
me." (p.22)

What little depth there is to Nesta is unpleasant. Envious
of Alice's circle of moneyed, secure, *married* people, Nesta
takes some highly questionable steps to snare some of those
goods for herself--or perhaps only to inform her penny-pinching,
dreary life with some romance. Alice's brother, Hugo, for instance, reluctantly reports:

> Your little Nesta had an eye for the men. . . . She made a pass
> at me once. . . . She'd been baby-sitting for us and I drove her
> home. She said would I see her into the shop because she was ner-
> vous in the dark. You know how slow and languid she was. There
> wasn't much in it but she sort of swayed against me in the dark.
> I put out my arm to stop her falling and she--well, she took hold
> of me and said she was so miserable, I mustn't leave her alone. I
> yanked her upstairs, put all the lights on and got out double-
> quick. (p. 66)

But Nesta doesn't take dismissal easily; thereafter, "she'd
talk to me as if we'd had a full-blown affair and had to be
kind of--well, keep it a secret. She kept saying Jackie

[Hugo's wife] mustn't ever know. But there wasn't anything *to* know." (p. 67) Indeed, to her surprise and dismay, the more Alice learns about this other side of Nesta's personality, the more motives to do away with her are revealed, each one of them incriminating someone dear to Alice herself.

Alice's final discovery shocks her fully as much as the belief that Nesta has been murdered shocks her, for, ultimately, someone points out that actually, except for differences in height, poise, compassion, and, of course, the accessories money can buy, Alice and Nesta resemble one another. During the climax of the novel--the moments of highest tension in her search and in the depths of her self-doubt--Alice even alters her appearance so as to accentuate the likeness. "I don't think I was quite conscious of what I was doing. I didn't know there was a resemblance till tonight. Perhaps I thought . . . Oh, I was so wretchedly unhappy . . . I must have thought if I copied her I'd succeed just as she had." (pp. 182-183)

In this moment of crisis, Alice is forced to the painful understanding that Nesta serves not only as a substitute for the child Alice has never had but also as a substitute for the fragile woman Alice has never been. The irony--and there is always an informing irony in Rendell's work--is that in her wish to be Nesta-like, Alice has really been seeking to be a lesser person, to be a leaner instead of a nurturer, to be a parasitic flower instead of a flourishing plant. Nesta represents what Alice might have become had her character been less strong, the potentially dark underside of Alice's personality. The reader, with Alice's friends, is left to hope that, now that she has learned some difficult truths about herself and her undeserving friend, Alice will develop a clear sense of her own worth.

Throughout *In Sickness and in Health*, Alice Fielding seeks to unravel not only a mystery of circumstance and event, but also a mystery of personality. She must face and renounce what she believes herself to be; face and reject the lesser person she might have been; and face and accept the decent, loving, potentially vibrant woman she is capable of being. The development of this motif lends depth and strength to Ruth Rendell's version of the conventional missing-person story.

*   *   *

At first glance, there seems to be little in common between Arthur Johnson and Anthony Johnson of *A Demon in My View* apart from the similarity in their names and the fact that they happen to live in the same London building. Arthur, as Rendell immediately makes known, is a psychopath, totally alienated from society. Anthony is a graduate student hoping to earn his doctorate in psychopathy and is so favorably disposed toward society that he undertakes volunteer work among the children in the neighborhood. Yet, as the startling plot develops, it becomes clear to the reader that the men share a surprising number of characteristics; in fact, they are two facets of one personality. Arthur demonstrates what Anthony might have become had circumstances been different, and Anthony begins to exhibit some of Arthur's traits when his personal tensions become almost overwhelming.

Both men have been defined by women who have exercised

profound influences over their lives. Arthur has been reared
by his Auntie Gracie who literally bought him from his natural
mother when he was an infant. During Arthur's youth, the two
lived together in seeming harmony, ruled by Auntie Gracie's
strict concepts of what makes the respectable life and by
Arthur's keen desire to be worthy of both his purchase price
and of Gracie's frequently stressed efforts.

> Once he had protested that he didn't need an umbrella to walk
> twenty yards through light rain or a hat to withstand ten min-
> utes' chill or a scarf against the faintly falling snow. But
> now he knew better. By keeping silent he could avoid hearing
> the words that aroused in him impotent anger and shame: "And
> when you get ill like you were last time, I suppose you'll ex-
> pect me to work myself into the ground nursing you and waiting
> on you." (p. 132)

In contrast, the reader learns little about Anthony's
early life, but Rendell does make clear that he has recently
undergone a major change. He has been awakened to a new sense
of himself and the world around him, having fallen in love
with Helen Garvist, a married woman who has aroused a sense of
wonder within him. Through Helen's softening, sensitizing influence, Anthony has overlaid his pragmatism with an aura of
romance, and she has taught him the habit of introspection.

Life with these influential women is not entirely smooth
for either Arthur or Anthony; Arthur is so constantly plauged
with a sense of failure that his love for Auntie Gracie and
his relationships with all other women are severely impaired:
"She had never been very pleased with him, had she? He had
never reached those heights of perfection she had laid before
him as fitting for one who needed to cleanse himself of the
taint of his birth and background." (pp. 15-16) Indeed, he is
so sexually inhibited that he has twice, years before the
story opens, sought release in murdering unknown women he encounters on the street. Unremorseful but concerned about his
own safety, Arthur has latterly sublimated his murderous sexual
drive by repeatedly "strangling" a shop window dummy he has
found in the cellar of the apartment house. Significantly, he
has dressed her in his dead aunt's clothing.

> She should save him, she should be--as those who would like to get
> hold of him would call it--his therapy. The women who waited in
> the dark streets, asking for trouble, he cared nothing for them,
> their pain, their terror. He cared, though, for his own fate. To
> defy it, he would kill a thousand women in her person, she should
> be his salvation. And then no threat could disturb him. (pp.
> 13-14)

Arthur has realized that he cannot lead an ordinary life.
If he frequents dark streets or allows himself even a little
liquor, he fears, he will murder again. Powerless in the grip
of first his aunt and then her memory, Arthur creates for himself a tiny, safe, obsessively controlled world, moving by
daylight to and from his dreary job and compulsively glorying
in the Auntie-Gracie-like neatness of his flat. For sexual
release, he has his mannequin; for the very limited amount of
human contact he desires, he has his television set.

Anthony, in initial contrast, has just expanded his life.

Frustrated with Helen's inability to leave her husband and come to him, he has moved to London to work on his doctoral dissertation and to force her to make a choice. Their communications are limited; he phones her once a week when her husband is out, and she writes him. Impatient for her decision and fearful lest she opt for the conventional and stay with her husband, he seeks relief in his studies and in helping the local children prepare for Guy Fawkes Day. Quickly accepted by his neighbors and the parents of the children, he provides them with the mannequin he's found in the cellar and thus entwines his life completely with Arthur's, for the guy, the mannequin, is burned in a glorious bonfire. In expanding his own world, Anthony has destroyed Arthur's safety valve.

Arthur seeks vengeance and gains it by destroying Helen's letters, the major link between the lovers: "Arthur felt a surge of power. Just as the control of his destiny, his peace, had lain in Anthony Johnson's hands, so the other man's now lay in his. An eye for an eye, a tooth for a tooth. Anthony Johnson had taken away his white lady; now he would take from Anthony Johnson *his* woman, rob him as he had been robbed of his last chance." (p. 79)

Arthur's recourses, further murder and his revenge on Anthony, occupy the central action of the book, for the main plot focuses upon him and his behavior. But underscoring the tense irony of the men's involvement with one another is a second, subtler plot which depicts Anthony's reaction to the deprivation and frustration. Even before Arthur takes action, Anthony has warned Helen that he will not wait much longer: "Your next letter is going to be very important, maybe the most important letter you'll ever write. . . . I'm sick to death of being kicked around, and it'll soon be too late." (p. 65) Later, believing himself to have been summarily rejected, he writes a furious letter. "Helen should learn she couldn't dismiss him as if he were some guy she'd picked up and spent a couple of nights with." (p. 126)

His reaction is so sharp that Anthony begins to worry about his ability to keep things in any sort of perspective: "It is very easy to become paranoid in certain situations, to believe that the whole world is against you. But what if the whole world, or those significant members of it, truly are against you?" (p. 129) His sense of alienation and his loss of perspective are particularly alarming to the careful reader who remembers Anthony's important reaction to Arthur's mannequin:

> He went up to the model, staring curiously at the battered face and the great rent in its neck. Then, hardly knowing why, he touched its cold smooth shoulders. Immediately his fingertips seemed again to remember the feel . . . of fine warm flesh, and he realized how hungry he had been to touch a woman. There was something obscene about the figure in front of him, that dead mockery of femaleness with its pallid hard carapace as cold as the shell of a reptile and its attenuated unreal limbs. He wanted to knock it down and leave it to lie on the sooty floor, but he restrained himself and turned quickly away. The others were waiting for him. (p. 62)

Frustrated and angry, Anthony reacts bitterly in several ways. He begins to reject the gift of expanded awareness that

Helen has given him: "He told himself that her quotations and her whole Eng. Lit. bit bored him." (p. 135) Also, like Arthur, Anthony seeks to assuage his frustration by substituting another woman for the object of his love and his despair:

> Love is the cure for love. Anthony knew that whatever might happen between him and Linthea it could at best be a distraction. But what was wrong with distractions? His love for Helen had been deep, precious, special. It was absurd to suppose that that could be replaced at will. But many activities and many emotions go under the name of love, and almost any one of them will for a while divert the mind from the real, true, and perfect thing. (p. 134)

Just as Arthur has lived twenty years in a confined, tiny world, so Anthony now begins to shut out the larger world about him. A local murder (Arthur has struck again) and the courtship between two good friends offer him little distraction:

> The police hunt afforded him no interest, brought him no curiosity. Nothing was able to divert him from the all-enclosing grey misery which had succeeded disbelief, anger, pain. The wedding . . . had served only to vary his depression with fresh pain. And in the airport lounge, where they sat drinking coffee, a horrible aspect of that pain had shown itself. For that busy place, with its continual comings and goings, was peopled for him with Helens, with versions of Helen. Every fair head, turned from him, might turn again and show him her face. One girl, from a distance, had her walk; another, talking animatedly to a man . . . moved her hands in Helen's gestures, and her laugh, soft and clear, reached him as Helen's laugh. Once he was certain. He even got to his feet, staring, catching his breath. The others must have thought him crazy, hallucinated. (pp. 161-162)

Like Arthur, Anthony has become obsessive, and, disturbing as this reaction is, another is perhaps even more alarming. He begins to project his anger toward Helen onto other women, and his reactions are sometimes very nearly violent. During his friends' wedding celebration, he is the object of the overtures of a flirtatious girl who lives in the same building and whose ability to play one suitor against another is well known to all the occupants. Furious at her, furious at Helen, furious at his sense that women are selfish manipulators, Anthony lashes out. "He wondered afterwards if he would actually have struck her, at least have given her a savage push, had Winston not interrupted." (p. 154)

Because Anthony symbolizes the normal world, a world populated with men and women who control their emotions and who have been socialized to respond to tension in a civilized manner, his decline toward violence is extremely disturbing. Anthony represents the reader, and Rendell suggests through this character's development that perhaps any human being is capable of total loss of control.

Further, Anthony's decline is responsible for one of the story's great ironies. Preoccupied almost totally with himself, he has failed to notice Arthur's true personality, despite the fact that all of London is now searching for him and the publicity is intense. The pressures to which Anthony is being subjected are so great that his professional skills as

well as his personal controls are jeopardized. But unlike
Arthur, Anthony is a civil person and a trained professional,
and, to the reader's great relief, these qualities finally reassert themselves. Furthermore, because Anthony's character
is realistic, complex, and essentially well integrated, his
ultimate awareness of his lapse is also the moment of his
greatest use of Helen's gift of insight and empathy:

> He knew now. He would have laughed at himself if this had been
> a laughing matter, for the irony was that he who was writing a
> thesis on psychopathy, who knew all about psychopaths, had lived
> three months in the same house as a psychopath and not known it.
> . . . Knew? Did he? Well, he was sure, certain. When we say
> that, Helen had once said, we always mean we are not quite sure,
> not quite certain. He shivered in the hot, stuffy yet draughty
> room. It had been a shock. Presently he began looking through
> his books, finding Arthur Johnson or aspects of him in every case
> history, finding what he well knew already. . . .
> At last he undressed and got into bed. . . . He found it im-
> possible to sleep and wondered if the man upstairs, lying in bed
> some twenty feet above him, also lay sleepless under his far
> greater weight of care. (p. 173)

Anthony has learned the lessons of his profession and Hel-
en's lessons of empathy well, after all, and having taught her
reader to identify with Anthony and to question his own control through Anthony, Rendell now offers some comfort and hope.
If Anthony can regain his self-control even while believing
Helen to be lost, if his professional training can reassert
itself, and if he can empathize with an unloved and unloving
person such as Arthur, there is, perhaps, hope for the ordinary
reader who, like Anthony, is subject to lapses but is nevertheless committed to civilizing principles.

* * *

A Demon in My View demonstrates that Anthony Johnson's
quest for his version of the Trojan woman has been arduous; in
seeking her he has almost lost himself. Like Alice Fielding
in *In Sickness and in Health,* he has been forced to study another person and through that observation has learned some
disagreeable things about himself. Both characters are the
better for their experiences, and the similarity of pattern
between the two novels reveals some useful insights into Rendell's development as a writer.
In Sickness and in Health is an interesting book, and,
early as it comes in the canon, it indicates Rendell's ability
to experiment with an established formula. But while the
characterizations of Alice and Nesta are fully adequate, they
appear a shade thin when compared to the later characterizations of Anthony and Arthur. In all ways, *A Demon in My View*
is the better book, more complex, more original, more fully
controlled. The comparison of the two novels, then, illus-
trates that Rendell has come to undertake authorial problems
of greater and greater difficulty and that she handles them
with growing skill.
Rendell has also progressed in her examination of human
nature. The portraits of Alice and Nesta reveal an author who
understands and can depict a good deal about human personal-

(Continued on page 32)

It's About Crime

By Marvin Lachman

BUSINESS AND THE MYSTERY STORY

"The business of America is business."
—Calvin Coolidge

Much has been written about the mysteries of Emma Lathen;
they do a superb job of satirizing Wall Street. At their best,
e.g. *Murder Against the Grain* and *When in Greece*, they are good
mysteries, too. Otherwise, few mysteries have done a good job
of integrating the world of business into the mystery, but a
trio of books, all of which, coincidentally, were Edgar win-
ners, are notable exceptions.

The murder victim in Alan Green's *What a Body!* (1949),
Merlin Broadstone, is clearly based on Bernarr McFadden, a
nationally known health faddist. Broadstone ("The Caliph of
Calisthenics . . . the Dictator of Diet") is bumped off in the
very first paragraph of Green's book, as he prepares to launch
a new health resort hotel.

What a Body! satirizes U.S. business and everything else
that is not nailed down, including sexual mores and national
politics. For example, a southern senator is questioned by
the police as a suspect. He says, "I've never seen a state
like this. Out my way we're foursquare. We either accuse a
man and lynch him or we let him go. I don't like all this
nervous shilly-shally."

There are two reasons to read every word of *What a Body!*
First, it's a fair-play mystery with enough suspects and
physical clues to make it possible to guess the murderer. I
didn't, however. Second, Green is a funny writer, and by
skipping you run the risk of missing some clever lines. Example: A detective following a suspect in a hotel is too late
to intercept him before he gets into an elevator. The detective dashes into the adjoining elevator and tells the operator,
"Follow that car."

During the 1940's and 1950's, the United States had a
fascination with the advertising industry. The jargon of
Madison Avenue became a subject of derision--everywhere but
on Madison Avenue. Sartorial terms like "Gray Flannel" and
"Button Down" took on adjectival lives of their own. Henry
Slesar's *Gray Flannel Shroud* (1959) has a lot going for it--
including the author's first-hand experience as an advertising

copywriter.

The chapter headings, anticipating Lathen, are clever, making use of advertising slogans then current, such as "The skin you love to touch" and "It's shot from guns." It's a book of many surprises and twists, with an ending which is legitimate, if a slight letdown. The hero, Dave Robbins, is intelligent and likable. If a film version is ever made, Alan Alda would be perfect for the part.

There is, as a bonus, a quotation which rings home with deadly truth to those of us who work a five-day week: "Tuesday was the worst day. Tuesday didn't have the numbing effect of Monday, the middle-of-the-week solidity of Wednesday, the hopeful face of Thursday, the home-stretch feel of Friday. Tuesday was the worst, and Dave woke in a tangle of steamy sheets to the idea that this Tuesday would cap them all."

Chaucer was never better.

William De Andrea also uses clever quotations to head his chapters, but his are taken from television, e.g. "Now let's see what terrific prize is waiting for you behind that door" and "To boldly go where no man has gone before." He mildly kids the television industry (calling the headquarters building of a TV network "the Tower of Babble"), but he is basically a defender of commercial TV. In fact, his polemic praising it is a paean in the ass.

Still, De Andrea's *Killed in the Ratings* (1978) is amusing, tells a good, fast-moving story, and introduces a hero, Matt Cobb, whom I'd like to hear from again.

NOTES ON RECENT READING

There are just too many new (and old) books to read in one lifetime. During the night I seem to hear plaintive cries from my book shelves, "Read me!" "No, read *me* first." Sorry, boys and girls, I'm doing the best I can.

There has been a lot of worthwhile stuff recently, in addition to the three "business" novels discussed above. Harper's Perennial Library remains in the forefront with two good books almost every month. Especially noteworthy are reprints of three 1955 books. Thomas Sterling's *Evil of the Day* is set in Venice and does a splendid job of evoking that city--and of telling a good story, too. Not surprising, when one remembers that Sterling is one of the best travel writers around. I hope that some day soon a publisher will reprint his *House Without a Door* (1950), about a recluse finding murder when she leaves her apartment for the first time in thirty-four years.

Another Perennial reprint is Henry Wade's novel, *A Dying Fall*. Wade is an author who doesn't deserve to be forgotten, but virtually no one reads him any more. Perhaps being in paperback will restore him to the place in the field that Sayers, Barzun and Taylor, and Shibuk rightly felt he had earned. Wade was near the end of his career (at age sixty-eight) when this book was published. It's a fine detective story with a good picture of post-war Britain and some nicely ironic touches. Wade is eminently readable.

Even better than Andrew Garve (whom he resembles in subject matter and anti-Communist conviction) is Robert Harling

in *The Enormous Shadow*, yet another book from that wonderful
year of 1955. If there is a better spy novel of the Cold War,
I haven't read it. It is a civilized book, and yet tension
mounts steadily, culminating in a breathtaking finale on the
River Thames.

Because his series detective, Dave Branstetter, is unique
in mystery fiction (I exempt George Baxt's Pharoah Love, who
is not worth regarding seriously), many people have heard of
Joseph Hansen's mysteries without reading them. They know Brandstetter is a homosexual, but they do not know how good the
books about him are. The good news is that they are very good
indeed and finally available in quality paperback editions in
Holt, Rinehart and Winston's Owl Book series. Incidentally,
has anyone else noted how many publishers use birds and beasts
in their colophons? Some day, whether or not there is any de-
mand for it, I plan to do a compendium of these.

But I digress. The five Brandstetter novels that have
been published are: *Fadeout* (1970), $2.95; *Death Claims* (1973),
$2.95; *Troublemaker* (1975), $3.50; *The Man Everybody Was Afraid
Of* (1978), $3.50; and *Skinflick* (1979), $2.95. Based on my
reading of the first book, this is a worthwhile series, and
one to read chronologically. Brandstetter is a fully realized
person who, in addition to searching for a missing (presumed
dead) singer, must cope with a crisis in his love life.

Hansen, like most writers of Southern California mysteries,
uses too many metaphors, but a high percentage of his are successful, drawing good word pictures. He catches the flavor of
the area, and he paints his characters clearly and truly.

There are signs that Ed McBain is getting tired of the
87th Precinct, but publishers are not. Ballantine has just
reprinted *Killer's Choice* (1958), $2.25, one of the early
books in the series. It's absorbing and fast-moving, though
it contains no great surprises. A much later book is *Ghosts*
(1980), $2.25, from Bantam. *Ghosts* is recommended by Stephen
King as the best in the whole series. That plug is bound to
increase sales, but it is without basis. Perhaps it was caused
by McBain's gratuitous use of the occult. "Best of the series"?
Ghosts is a strong contender for worst. If you want to read
the best 87th Precinct novel, try *The Heckler* (1960), in which
Carella and company come up against a genuine master criminal.
I don't recall seeing it in paperback since the Permabook reprint in 1961, but a word to the wise publisher should be suf-
ficient.

MYSTERY NEWS

1. The troubled, abandoned Francis Coppola production of *Hammett* may make the screen after all. Ross Thomas has completed
a new film script for it, and filming is to resume early in
November 1981, with completion expected by the end of the year.
Thomas has also done the script for *Sweat Shop*, which Coppola
is doing as a two-part NBC "Movie of the Week."

2. John Franklin Bardin, best known for his mysteries which
dealt with abnormal psychology, died in New York City on July
9 at the age of sixty-four. Bardin had also been an editor

and had done advertising and publicity work. He wrote seven
mysteries, three under his own name, one as by Douglas Ashe,
and three as by Gregory Tree.

3. Fans of folk music probably know Lee Hays as one of the co-
founders of the famous singing group, "The Weavers." They may
not realize that he had three short stories published in EQMM
between 1948 and 1954. He died on August 26 at age sixty-seven.

(Continued from page 2) to Gravesend Books, Box 235, Pocono
Pines, PA 18350. Even if you don't buy books by mail, this
beautifully printed, sixty-four-page catalogue belongs on your
reference shelf.

I've already gone on at too great length this time, but
there are still a few other things I must mention. Harald
Mogensen advises that he and Tage la Cour will have a completely
revised edition of their excellent *Murder Book* out next year,
which is news of the best sort. And Jane Bakerman has asked
me to pass along some information regarding the joint convention of the Popular Culture and the American Culture Associa-
tions, to be held in Louisville, Kentucky, April 14-18, 1982.
Jane is the chairperson for the mystery/detection sessions,
and she wanted me to pass along her invitation to you all to
propose papers for presentation on the program. Unfortunately,
her deadline was November 5, which is long past, but if any of
you would like information on the convention you can write to
Jane at the Department of English, Indiana State University,
Terre Haute, IN 47809

One last thing. There is no Bouchercon report in this
issue, but, if enough of us write threatening letters to John
Nieminski, perhaps he'll write one up in time for the next TMF.

(Continued from page 20) annuals. Sapphire and Steel have
appeared in one book (entitled *Sapphire and Steel*) by Peter
T. Hammond, published as an original Star paperback in 1979.
It is in fact a novelisation of the first television serial--
about a haunted house in which the parents of two children
disappear and nursery rhymes seem to come gruesomely to life.

(Continued from page 28) ities under stress and who can, further, raise serious questions about the human condition. The
progression in Ruth Rendell's development as a writer and in
the intricacy of her product is both admirable and enormously
gratifying to the reader, for it demonstrates that she is one
contemporary novelist who regards crime fiction as a serious
art. This attitude puts her in the company of such highly
regarded authors as Charles Dickens and Ross Macdonald and
indicates that she is clearly worthy of serious critical attention.

William Hughes. *Split on Red*. Wyndham/Moat Hall, 1979, 225 pp.

It was George Kelley--a name you should know--who recommended this book to me. In fact, he says the whole series is
worth trying to obtain. This is the first of four adventures
of PI George Willis to have been published so far, all in
England.

Now, as you may have noticed, there are some books that
George and I have in essence agreed to disagree on--most of
the recent Spenser novels, for example--but while I'm not as
enthusiastic as George seems to be, I think he has something
here.

That all four books are paperback originals may help explain why no U.S. publisher has picked up on them. And they
are different. George Willis is not fully hard-boiled, at
least not at the beginning of the book, though by the end of
this first case he certainly has come close to it. There is
plenty of sex involved, including some on the kinky side--with
handcuffs, yet--and at one point he starts whipping a suspect
to get the truth from her, until he discovers that she is only
enjoying it.

And before he's done he's killed any number of Arabs
(mostly) who've gotten in his way. The case begins with a
missing girl, and it continues on into a fine, glorious mixture of pornography, oil wells, and international diplomacy.

Willis, cast out from the police and a loner by nature,
flounders more than I thought he should have, but he wraps it
all up in the end in a classical final confrontation with all
the possible (remaining) suspects all in the same room.

I'll probably read the other three very soon now. (B)

H.R.F. Keating. *Go West, Inspector Ghote*. Doubleday/Crime
Club, 1981, 182 pp., $9.95.

In commenting on *The Murder of the Maharaja*, the book
Keating wrote immediately before this one, I suggested it as
the ideal candidate for the annual Agatha Christie Award, if
there was one.

There's no John Dickson Carr Award for the year's best
locked-room detective story, either, and it's a shame, for
here's a book that would be an odds-on favorite for this year's

prize.

In his latest book, Keating returns to his long-time series
character, Inspector Ganesh V. Ghote, of the Bombay C.I.D. The
puzzle concerns the mysterious death of a swami known to have
been alone in his empty house. For comic relief there is an
overbearing (and grossly overweight) American private eye, who
gives Ghote an unwanted and unwelcomed helping hand. And,
just as Carr often did himself, Keating stirs in more than a
hint of the supernatural as well.

Ghote, not so incidentally, is in the United States for
this case, on the trail of a young girl from India who has apparently succumbed to the charms of a Hindu-Californian yogi
with a life-style to match. Dazed by a mind-numbing culture
shock at first, the meek, self-effacing Ghote at length rises
to the occasion.

Providing most of the charm of this offbeat sort of detective story is the overwhelming contrast developed between
Ghote's two worlds, Bombay and Los Angeles.

It's just too bad that the solution to the puzzle has to
deflate the effect so considerably, although perhaps not fa-
tally. I remain with the feeling that a completely thorough
police search would have revealed the secret of the yogi's
strange death right away. (A minus)* (*Reviews so marked
have appeared earlier in the Hartford *Courant*.)

E.R. Punshon. *Mystery Villa*. Penguin, 1950, 220 pp.; first
published in 1934.

Written in the days when Sergeant Bobby Owen, Punshon's
long-running series character, was young and throbbing with
ambition and energy, this small puzzle of the mysterious,
reclusive lady of Tudor Lodge is a tiny little mystery that
grows and grows and grows.

But slowly! It is over fifty pages before Bobby finds
reason enough to investigate within, and in doing so he widens
the case forty or fifty years into the past--to a happy event
that never took place, and to a murder that did.

(Sorry to be so ambiguous. Part of the soporific pleasure
of reading this novel is just relaxing and letting events flow
over you, and I hope I haven't already said too much and de-
prived you of that particular enjoyment.)

The characters are nicely drawn--save Bobby, who has no
personal life to speak off, and otherwise is described completely by the first sentence of this review. Outdated, but
drawn with precision and care.

It is the detective work that fails to hold up, beginning
with a sloppy search of the house by the police themselves,
and continuing as Bobby completely forgets about one of the
characters involved. And of course that person turns out to
be the, um, well, yes, I shouldn't even say that, should I?

Overall, the worst crime a detective story can perpetrate
is that of being unconvincing. What with faulty premises, unlikely motivations, and sheer, devout wrongheadedness, well
. . . it's not really that bad, but . . . . (C)

Ross Thomas. *The Mordida Man*. Simon & Schuster, 1981, 284
pp., $13.95.

A terrorist with connections to Libya is kidnapped. The Libyans think the CIA was responsible, and so they take the president's brother as a hostage. They lop off his ear and send it to the president, who calls in the Mordida Man.

Who is Chubb Dunjee, an ex-congressman who received his nickname in Mexico for his ability to make a bribe count. He still has a reputation for setting events in motion.

Complications ensue. Thomas provides some very oblique tangents to what otherwise would be a fairly direct story, and he has it all firmly under control until the final minutes, when the plot suddenly seems to fall apart on him.

Don't try to analyze Chubb's final plan. It's too elaborate to have been improvised on the spot, which is his specialty. It obviously wasn't, and yet there appears to have been no way he could have known what to expect ahead of time. Plots as tightly wound as this one need airtight support. This one sags badly.

There's a lot to like in what comes before. Thomas is unarguably a witty and clever writer. Somehow, though, I seem this time to have left all my ardor in my other pants. (C plus)

William Kaye. *Wrong Target*. Leisure, 1981, 208 pp., $1.95.

You might call this a private-eye procedural. Not in the Joe Gores/DKA Agency sense, though, for I get the distinct impression that the closest William Kaye ever came to a real-life private investigator was about the same as you or I. In print, that is. From reading about them.

But in deciding to write about the adventures of a PI named Chickie French, Kaye probably made the right decision, since, if anything, he is even less apt at describing how real-life police operate.

For example, after French's sister, the wife of mayoral candidate Whit Davidson, is shot and killed at a political rally (note the title), French comes in late and still manages to get in his share of interrogating the witnesses. And when he's done, he and Davidson simply drive away. Methinks the cops clamp down harder than that, even in small towns.

Returning, though, to my original thoughts, French does do a neat job of shuffling several cases around at the same time--some of them are completely followed through on, some not; some are connected, some are not--and he still manages to squeeze in some time to solve his sister's murder.

Although I am still wondering about his secretary's strange behavior in chapter four--it is simply not referred to again at all--there are some very good moments here, many of them when French is being deeply nostalgic and introspective.

Unfortunately, it is not much of a mystery. Apparently Mr. Kaye has no sense of misdirection at all.

So, the book is terribly uneven and, yes, even amateurish in style and technique. However, the moments that are very good suggest that as a writer Kaye does have some promise. (On the other hand, whoever it was who wrote the copy for the back cover is simply and utterly incompetent. There's no other word for it.) (C minus)

E.V. Cunningham. *The Case of the Sliding Pool*. Delacorte

Press, 1981, 178 pp., $10.95.

On page one we are told that Masao Masuto is a Zen Buddhist. On page two, that he is a Nisei, which means that he was born in the U.S. of Japanese parents. And on page three we learn that, when called upon, he serves as half of the homicide squad of the Beverly Hills police force. He's a complex character, and it shows.
This is not his first case, and if, like me, you haven't read any of them, you'll want to go back and dig out his first three. In the one at hand, heavy rains sweep away a huge concrete swimming pool, leaving behind the burial ground of what now is nothing more than a thirty-year-old skeleton.
Faced with this challenge, Detective Sergeant Masuto immediately reconstructs the crime that must have taken place. Forthcoming are some of the most imaginative deductions since the days of Sherlock Holmes. (Or should that be Charlie Chan, whom Masuto is most often accused by his colleagues of emulating?
As it turns out, his theories, based on what seems to be little more than educated guesswork, not surprisingly do have some gaps in them. Masuto, however, while not as overly modest in regard to his abilities as an Inspector Ghote, say, is also not too proud to change his working hypotheses as he goes.
If it were not for the sudden, unexpected bombshell Cunningham explodes on the reader on page 152, wholly unanticipated and completely changing the direction of Masuto's investigation, this would have had to have been ranked as one of the top detective novels of the year.
The book is still terrifically readable, but you'll feel like giving Cunningham a kick in the spot where he most deserves it for all the holes that are left behind when he's finished. (B)*

Douglas Clark. *Roast Eggs*. Dodd, Mead, 1981, 175 pp., $8.95.

Of necessity, Superintendent Masters is called in on this case, but it's almost too late for what appears to be a losing cause. In the final days of the trial of a man accused of burning down his house--with his wife unfortunately still inside--the case for the prosecution is going badly.
The problem is that the husband has acquitted himself very nicely on the stand, and, what is worse, he has no obvious motive. Could he be innocent? The pieces of the puzzles must be reshuffled at once, and then juggled and rejuggled around until at last the truth emerges. And then, the question is, is there any time left to prove it?
As an exercise in creative and logical hypothesizing, nothing published in recent times seems to come close to rivaling this nifty little mystery-in-reverse. If your care is for characters who come to life, however, the only ones who ever do are the killer and his victim--and then it's only indirectly, in the last-ditch analysis of the case performed so furiously and dramatically by the nearly faceless members of the police and prosecution, hidden away in their smoke-filled deliberations room. (B plus)*

Vechel Howard. *Murder with Love*. Gold Medal, 1959, 125 pp.

Vechel Howard is not, I strongly suspect, a name that most
mystery readers will ever have at the tips of their tongues.
I know of only five books that have been published under that
by-line, and three of them are westerns. The title of the
other mystery is *Murder on Her Mind*, and it was published by
Gold Medal just about the same time as this one. It's buried
somewhere downstairs in the basement, though, and right now I
can't tell you if private eye Johnny Church, the hero of the
book at hand, is also in that one. Hubin doesn't say.
Well, I'll stop teasing you. If you don't already know,
you may be as surprised as I was when I learned that Vechel
Howard is actually--are you ready for this?--Howard Rigsby.
There. I told you it would be a surprise.
Church may be one of those PI characters who get so involved in their one and only case there's no chance they'll
ever be in another book. The scene is Las Vegas, where his
client wants him to find a woman. He's not the only one,
either. Mira, as Church soon discovers, has had an uncontrollable habit of getting men to fall in love with her and then
taking off with all the money and expensive gifts bestowed
upon her, disappearing as mysteriously as she suddenly appeared.
This time, however, Church finds that blackmail, never
part of her game before, has been added to her repertoire--and
can murder be far behind? Church also stumbles across a pair
of delectable twin sex kittens, but he's really the kind of
guy who gets hit over the head a lot and goes to bed with nobody. Almost.
The action is standard enough. It's the ending which is
unusual. A bit maudlin as well, perhaps, but it's the kind
that lingers on. Longer, in fact, than the story itself.
(B minus)

H. Paul Jeffers. *Rubout at the Onyx*. Ticknor & Fields, 1981,
178 pp., $10.95.

Here is a private-eye story, but by no means is it your
common, everyday sort of private-eye story. Instead, it's a
swinging trip into the past, an excursion by make-believe time
machine into yesterday, back to the post-Prohibition, jazz-era
days of the Big Apple's "Cradle of Jazz"--Fifty-second Street,
that is, between Fifth and Sixth. The year, 1935.
The private eye is Harry MacNeil. His office is located
upstairs over the Onyx Club, the heart of the jazz district.
His client is a lately bereaved widow. Her husband was a two-
bit gangster who was rubbed out downstairs on New Year's Eve.
She brings Harry a message in code that may lead them to a
three million dollar fortune in stolen diamonds. She is also
a little lonely.
Balancing the two rather nicely, Jeffers never really
seems to commit himself all the way as to whether he's writing
a history first, or a mystery. Whatever it is in the end,
there's no doubt whatsoever that it's a lot more fun to puzzle
through than any classroom textbook anyone's ever been assigned
to read. Strictly as a mystery, though . . . , well, sad to
say, there's no great revelation that comes at the end. Mac-
Neil uncovers the truth by just plain diligence, and the cul-

prit is fairly obvious from a long way off. (B minus)*

Robert Barnard. *Death of a Perfect Mother*. Scribner's, 1981,
188 pp., $9.95

To tell the truth, as a second thought about the title
might tell you, Lill Hodsden is something less than perfect
as a mother and as a wife. She is the loud, vulgar type, the
victim of an over-indulgent self-love, and a haggard creature
of sexual cravings and wiles--or so she's pictured. It is no
wonder her two sons are planning to kill her.
Nor are they the only ones. Upon Lill's untimely passing,
the fatal victim of a "mugging" attack before her boys can do
more than plan, the spotlight falls on the motives of at least
a dozen others as well.
A detective story of sorts does come about as a result,
but it's a detective story simply steeped in large globs of
delightfully unmitigated cynicism. And contempt as well,
especially for middle-class conventions, as exemplified best
by the fairly incompetent inspector who's been placed in charge
of the case.
I don't really know the minimum daily requirement of well-
guided misanthropism in everyone's reading diet, but there
must be one, and Barnard seems to be cross enough at the world
for all of us. Most certainly, for all its inherent honesty,
this is not quite the book to be read and appreciated on
Mother's Day! (B)*

David E. Fisher. *Variation on a Theme*. Doubleday/Crime Club,
1981, 182 pp., $10.95.

When struggling playwright Henry Grace resumes a love affair he had with a woman he knew twenty years ago, he hardly
expects soon to be providing an iron-clad alibi for her hus-
band--especially when he knows without a doubt that the man is
the one responsible for the lady's death.
No, it wasn't a contract killing. The man really did it
himself, and, if it's not giving too much away, the deed was
done by a plan surprisingly too clever for the plot itself.
In fact, the killer's cleverness is appreciated the most only
after how he did it has finally been revealed. In most "impossible crimes"--locked-room murders and the like--telling
how usually seems to spoil the effect, but not here.
Fisher knows beans about standard police procedure, but I
can't see that it matters. His first attempt at a mystery
novel is simple and devious at the same time, and it swings in
a loose, easy, show-businessy sort of way. And just as the
crime is solved, the nightmare really begins for Henry Grace--
not the phoney-baloney stuff of the occult or the supernatural,
but the real terror of the real world, and just as dangerous.
This one's got a lot going for it, and I think it'll keep
you up for a while. (B plus)*

Ruth Rendell. *Death Notes*. Pantheon, 1981, 208 pp., $9.95.

Long-time fans of Ruth Rendell's Chief Inspector Wexford

simply will not want to miss this latest book in the series,
an example of superb plotting which harkens back to the glory
days of the 1930's and 40's and the greatest fictional detectives of all time. In *Death Notes*, Rendell and Wexford make
for a team just about impossible to beat.

Something has happened to Rendell's story-telling ability,
however. The story starts slowly, and the pace often seems
awkward, if not downright clumsy. The writing is heavy-handed
and stolidly unimaginative--paradoxically so, for someone capable of squeezing so much ingenuity into a criminal investigation.

As for the case itself, a wealthy man dies--of misadventure?
--and his only heir is a girl who claims to be his long-lost
daughter. Wexford is convinced she is not, and he finds himself so obsessed with proving her an imposter that he spends
his yearly vacation in California, tracing the girl's past
back even further.

As it turns out, the case is both more and less complex
than it seems. For the armchair detective at home, every bit
of the action, every small piece of information, is important.
Rendell is challenging each of her readers to a duel of wits,
and I'm willing to wager that she wins more often than she
loses. (B)*

Michael Z. Lewin. *Missing Woman*. Knopf, 1981, 213 pp., $10.95.

There are a number of top-notch candidates for the best
private-eye series going today. On the top of a good many
lists would be Robert B. Parker's Spenser books, but fans of
the more traditional PI yarn would probably go more for the
likes of Bill Pronzini's nameless detective or Arthur Lyons'
Jacob Asch stories.

Sometimes lost and passed over in the shouting is Albert
Samson, billed at one time as "the cheapest detective in In-
dianapolis." He's undoubtedly still cheap. At the beginning
of this book he is definitely broke, and about to be evicted
from his office as part of a big, downtown redevelopment project.

Which of course is not to say he's not honest, dependable,
and next to impossible to pry loose from a case. Even if he
sounds a bit sour on his life (not on life, just his), his
sense of humor never leaves him. Mostly it's of a subtle va-
riety, but not always, especially when he's irritated. His
relations with Lt. Powder of Missing Persons do seem to be
improving, however.

Luckily so, for, as you've already gathered from the title,
that's the kind of case this latest one is. Samson jumps in
with all abandon, treating it as the intellectual challenge it
is, when suddenly he's caught up with the abrupt realization
that Murder Is Not a Game.

Detective stories do tend to tread a thin line between
reality and fantasy. Michael Lewin's big achievement here may
very well be that he manages to give us the best of both. (A)*

John Weisman. *Evidence*. Signet, 1981, 248 pp., $2.95; first
published in 1980.

The half-life of current paperback fiction seems to be about two weeks these days, so I suspect that if you missed this when it came out it's going to be pretty hard to find. You won't find it mixed in with the mysteries, even though it was, I believe, nominated by the MWA as one of the best of the year. If they have it, your favorite bookstores are more likely to have it stuck in with the general fiction--led on, no doubt, by the large quote by Joseph Wambaugh in red letters on the cover.

And as everybody knows, Joseph Wambaugh doesn't write "mystery fiction."

But I think, in this case at least, that your favorite bookstore owner is going to know best. I don't think too many mystery fans are going to wax overly enthusiastic over the extra dimensions this book brings to, well, let's call it "crime fiction," shall we?

There is a crime involved, several of them to be precise, and of course murder is one of them. In the more immediate background, however, are the "organized" crimes of the heroin trade and prostitution--both male and female, but mostly the former, and the younger the better.

Graphic sex comes as a matter of course, of all varieties (but mostly the former, and the younger the better). On page seventy-seven one of the major characters pukes. You may want to as well, assuming, that is, that you decide this is a book you want to read to begin with.

I don't mean to scare you off. It's tough and it's un-compromising, but it's also as compellingly readable as they come. It's an inside look at the life of a veteran investi-gative reporter named Robert Mandel, and in Detroit he's got plenty to write about. He's also manic-obsessive about his work. Over the line.

His latest assignment has him tracking down the killers of another reporter--Mandel's closest friend on the paper, maybe his only friend. It's told as a rambling series of reminis-cences, but the point slowly becomes clear. As Mandel tells us about himself, and as he digs deeper and deeper into the homosexual underground of the Motor City and environs, more and more the reader comes to realize just how insanely cold and cynical this man is. He claims he's only an observer. He has no other goal than to gather evidence. That's his profes-sion.

The evidence he gathers has only one purpose, and that is not justice. It is the story he is writing. Nothing else matters. His friend Jack died because he broke the rules. That's all Mandel lives by. Sadly, it's all he has left. (A)

L.A. Morse. *The Old Dick.* Avon, 1981, 236 pp., $2.25.

There've been a number of detectives in the world of de-tective fiction whom you'd have to call "elderly," but at age seventy-eight I think Jake Spanner has most of them beat. Miss Marple was up in her eighties when she was still active, I think, and some of you with better memories than mine can probably come up with more right away.

But how many of these would you call hard-boiled private eyes? In his own words, Jake Spanner has always tried never to give satisfaction to assholes, if he could help it, and now that he's retired he sees no reason to change.

He hasn't had an erection in five years, either, or at least so he says at the beginning of chapter one. How old he is soon begins to sound like an obsession with him, but with old duffers like this, sometimes you just put up with things like that a little bit more.

Spanner comes out of retirement in this book, as you would have guessed, but throughout it all he remains pretty much surprised by it. At any rate, he decides to give a helping hand to a one-time enemy from the old days, a gangster known as Sal the Salami (for reasons we won't go into here). It seems that his grandson has been kidnapped, but, just as in a good Chandler novel, complications begin to develop and thrive, deliciously so.

I don't know who the author is. If someone were to tell me it's not his first book, that he's written loads of others, I wouldn't be surprised at all. L.A. Morse, whoever he is, has an inventive touch that adds tremendously to a rather familiar story, plus a consistent style and a slightly vulgar sense of humor to match.

There are some books in which you're lucky to get one of the above. (A minus)

Anthony Olcott. *Murder at the Red October*. Academy Chicago, 1981, 226 pp., $11.95.

There is a theory in the field of cultural anthropology which attempts to explain just why it is that a given idea seems to occur independently to several different people at the same time.

It has something to do with the tides of history and the concept that important scientific advances, for example, are inevitable conclusions to a preceding series of events, and it doesn't really matter who was the first to come up with an idea.

Although a "follow the leader" syndrome must obviously be watched for and guarded against, the same principle seems to apply to literature as well. Both this book and Stuart Kaminsky's *Death of a Dissident* (Ace/Charter, 1981) follow so closely upon the publication of Martin Cruz Smith's best-selling *Gorky Park* that it appears that the idea of a murder mystery taking place in Moscow was produced and replicated by forces other than pure emulation.

Whether these forces are the same as those that brought about Ronald Reagan's landslide victory in the recent presidential election remains a matter of additional speculation.

In the case at hand, the murder of a suspicious American tourist in the second-class Hotel Red October drives its night-time security officer, Ivan Palych Duvakin, into a nightmare world of black-marketing and heroin-trafficking. It causes his soft comfortable world to start crumbling around him, and yet at the same time it also gives him a brief hint of a better future coming.

Secondary to the mystery Duvakin is forced to unravel by his unsympathetic superiors is the utterly bleak picture that is painted of life in present-day Moscow. If Olcott, who has lived there for two years, is to be believed, Russia is eternally a land of bitter cold and constant shortages, and a

(Continued on page 48)

Verdicts
(More Reviews)

Geoffrey O'Brien. *Hardboiled America: The Lurid Years of
Paperbacks.* Van Nostrand Reinhold, 1981, 144 pp., $16.95.

Hardboiled is one label for it, but others fit just as
well: tawdry, sordid, hard-hitting, realistic, downbeat, *noir*.
Within this descriptive cluster falls a huge amount of the
American fiction that was mass-marketed in 25¢ paperback book
form in the fifteen years after World War II. Its protagonists are men and women of the lower depths--tough private
eyes, lone-wolf cops, loose women in tight skirts, gangsters,
juvenile delinquents, drunks, psychotics, people on the run.
Its primal scenes feature steamy sex and raw violence, and the
cover illustrations which the paperback publishers commissioned
for these books stressed such sequences in lurid colors. Some
of the stuff was reprinted from hardcover; more and more of
it, especially after 1950, was written expressly for the paperbacks. A lot was trash but a surprising amount, such as the
work of Hammett and Chandler and John D. MacDonald, was first-
rate writing by any standard. Whatever you thought of this
sort of book, if you came to maturity during that decade-and-
a-half you couldn't escape it. Dozens of these paperbacks
blazed out at you from metal racks wherever books were sold.
Poet Geoffrey O'Brien has captured the fascination with
both the prose and the graphics of the "hardboiled" era in
this loosely structured and lyrically written book. His mini-
essays on some of the writers who contributed to the genre--
not just household names like Mickey Spillane, but people like
Cornell Woolrich, David Goodis, and Jim Thompson, who are rec-
ognized in Europe as great *roman noir* authors yet sadly ne-
glected here--are models of insight, compression, and stylistic
fireworks. The text is backed up by dozens of reproductions
of typical paperback covers, many in their gloriously trashy
original colors.
O'Brien leaves out many unusually interesting softcover
specialists (William Ard, Michael Avallone, Day Keene, and
Harry Whittington among others) and makes an occasional factual
slip, such as misdating the Marlon Brando motorcycle movie *The
Wild One* by three years, but overall this is a marvelous object
lesson in how to write about popular culture with a keen critical eye, a strong, bright, quotable style, and a total absence
of academic pretentiousness. As history, as literary and cultural exploration, as nostalgia, *Hardboiled America* is a de-

light. (Francis M. Nevins, Jr.)

Dean R. Koontz. *How to Write Best Selling Fiction*. Writer's Digest Books, 1981, $13.95.

This controversial new writing manual includes a number of points I want to take issue with, specifically about the mystery field, but let me get some favorable comments out of the way first.

1) Koontz is a very good writer, and the facts and opinions he expresses make compelling reading for anyone interested in popular fiction, whether one actually wants to write it or not.

2) He is obviously sincere in his desire to help other writers, and the points he makes about plotting, style, characterization, grammar, contract-reading, and other professional matters are most worthwhile. I expect much of his advice to be of value in my own writing.

3) Although he covers some of the same areas here as in his earlier manual, *Writing Popular Fiction* (1972), and often refers to that book in the course of this one, this is a wholly new work rather than a glorified revision. Though it supersedes the earlier work in its view of the state of the market, both books belong on the shelves of writers.

4) Yes, read this book. It is one of the best-thought-out and most valuable how-to manuals on the market.

Now on to the cavils.

Koontz's championing of the mainstream (i.e. blockbuster) type of novel in this work, as opposed to the category of genre work he recommended to newcomers in his first book, parallels the development of his own career. Once a prolific science fiction novelist, he came to resent his typecasting in that category when he started writing "big" mainstream novels, even going to the extent of buying up rights to most of his sf to prevent it being reprinted. I do not question that switching to blockbusters was a viable commercial decision for Koontz and may be for many of his readers. What I object to is the idea implicit throughout his book that the blockbuster novel is superior to the genre novel by definition.

In a fine list of influential authors of contemporary popular fiction, Koontz credits successful writers who write solidly within genres or categories as having "transcended" the genre, the old Catch-22 that if you write a mystery or a western or a science fiction novel really well, you must actually be doing something else. Ross Macdonald, John D. MacDonald, Agatha Christie, Harry Kemelman, and others became best-seller-list successes writing solidly within the genre of detective fiction. Yet Koontz intimates that this is impossible.

He bewails the fact that Donald E. Westlake has never burst the bounds of the mystery field to move into mainstream novels. While such a move may have made Westlake more money, can we really assume that it would have created better art? Would Koontz contend that P.G. Wodehouse should have stopped writing his short comic novels in favor of 500-page bestseller candidates? The result probably would have been disastrous.

I am sure that I am just as bored as Koontz with novelists who write for English professors or an intellectual elite instead of trying to reach a broader range of readers. But that does not mean that I am willing to go with Koontz to the other

extreme that says what is most popular is necessarily best.
Taking that line of reasoning, you would have to say that the
best TV shows are the top ten in the ratings, a position few
people could find defensible.

The line Koontz preaches is part-and-parcel of the American equation of big with good. To Koontz, every novel attempt-
ed has to go for the homerun. The little novel is by definition a lesser novel. Though I would share Koontz's enthusiasm
for such "big book" crime writers as Lawrence Sanders and
Robert Ludlum, I would argue that most of the writers who try
to emulate their success would produce better books if they
tried for shorter, less ambitious "category" novels. Even
Sanders, a novelist whose worth Koontz and I agree on, would
have had a better (though doubtless not as money-making) book
in *The Second Deadly Sin* if he had written it half as long.

That the blockbusterites spend more time giving you details
about their characters does not necessarily mean, as Koontz
apparently believes, that they are doing better and deeper
characterizations. Some writers can bring a character more
fully to life in a couple of sentences than other writers can
do in a three-page biography-dossier.

It's hard for me to believe that Koontz would really hold
that the second-line blockbuster writers (or even most of the
first liners) were doing as good work in their inflated behe-
moth tomes as are writers like Charles Larson, Ruth Rendell,
Simon Brett, James McClure, Peter Dickinson, H.R.F. Keating,
Ellis Peters, Tony Hillerman, Jack S. Scott, or Michael Z.
Lewin when they work solidly within the bounds of the mystery
genre. Yet throughout the book, Koontz takes potshots at the
genre's barrenness of fresh voices, claiming that most of the
good new writers quickly move out of the ghetto and into the
camp of the blockbusterites.

Another of Koontz's controversial opinions is that the in-
cursion of the conglomerates into the book publishing field is
more beneficial than harmful to the industry. Though many will
disagree, he argues his point persuasively.

I can sum up my differences with Koontz in this way: If he
wants to claim going the blockbuster route is a more viable
commercial course for the new writer, he may well be right.
But in implying that the general run of mysteries puffed full
of air to "transcend" the genre are superior to the general
run of less pretentious mysteries of moderate length, he is
all wet. (Jon L. Breen)

Kenn Davis. *Dead to Rights*. Avon Books, 1981.

In the crime novel category, overladen with carnage, cor-
ruption, and greed, *Dead to Rights* must be at the top of the
class. Three almost-losers steal six million dollars worth of
negotiable bonds and plan to sell them at ten percent of face
value. But their buyer is planning her own double cross, and
the robbers are soon on their own in a snow-blocked city, pur-
sued by killers from the Organization and by the police. There
are no heroes here, the ending falls into place a bit too neatly, and there are a few unbelievable escapes and carryings-on-
while-wounded. In spite of that, the book has a drive and
compulsion that grabs you and keeps you panting along to the
last death. (Fred Dueren)

Max Collins. *Hush Money*. Pinnacle, 1981, $1.95.

Max Collins, who writes the Dick Tracy comic strip, has a
new Nolan crime caper out, the fourth in the series which Collins likes to call his "crook books."

The first three--*Bait Money*, *Blood Money*, and *Fly Paper*--
established Nolan as a strong individual who refused to kill a
friend who just happened to be romancing a Family member's
mistress. After the Family kills his friend, Nolan shoots the
guy who ordered the hit and stays on the run for fifteen years
because of an open contract on his life.

But that was all in the past, and now Nolan is a much
cooler fifty. Here the Family has a problem in Des Moines:
some psycho is killing off the local branch, the DiPreta
brothers. Chicago suspects a Vietnam vet who velieves the
DiPretas killed his mother. Nolan, once a family friend, becomes the logical peacemaker. He doesn't believe the Family's
story, but he goes out of a sense of duty.

The book combines a "crime procedural" theme (a logical
reversal of the popular police procedural) with a continuing
character study of Nolan and his twenty-one-year-old partner,
Jon, who loves comic books and women. The reader is helped
to suspend his dislike for organized crime by the tacit father-
son relationship between the two men, which shows that they do
have some redeeming qualities.

Collins' prose is clear, terse, and fast moving. The
chapters present the points of view of eight different characters, often overlapping the same action. The lean style
allows the reader to enjoy a type of crime story which, handled less professionally, would have been just another Mafia-
hitman story. *Hush Money* is an entertaining crime thriller
presented by one of the new masters in the field. (Jim Traylor)

James Melville. *The Wages of Zen*. Methuen Paperbacks, 1981,
175 pp., $4.25.

Apparently a first crime novel, *The Wages of Zen* introduces Superintendant Tetsuo Otani of the Hyogo Prefectural
Police. Studying in a rural Zen center called Chisho-Ji are
five foreigners, all Westerners. Superintendant Otani gets
word that there are illicit drugs at Chisho-Ji. What looks
like heroin is discovered among the belongings of Graham
Dillon, a Zen student from Ireland. Dillon knows nothing
about it. Soon after, the "heroin" is found to be talcum
powder and Dillon is found murdered, his head smashed. Murder
in Japan, it is explained, is rare unless related to gangland
warfare or intimate family matters.

Early on, as Otani and others investigate, several unexpected things are learned. The director of Chisho-Ji is
sexually promiscuous and has a bank account too large for a
Zen master; Dillon, the murder victim, turns out to have been
a Catholic priest; Japanese Security is interested in each of
the foreigners, two of whom are lesbians; and the center has
links to local gangland bosses.

These revelations are increasingly inconsistent with the
proper temper of life at a Zen study center, but Melville uses
them to provide a transition between a relatively quiet murder
at the beginning and a climax where we learn that, among other

things, Chisho-Ji has connections with international terrorism, and the CIA is involved.

This is supposed to be a police procedural. We get to know something of Otani's character and home life. He even reads *krimi* novels and compares himself unfavorably to Maigret and Van der Valk. But Otani never directs or coordinates the investigation. In fact, what little detection we see is done by Otani's subordinates, largely independent of his knowledge. As more and more facts are uncovered, the narrative switches viewpoints more and more frequently, and Otani slips from the picture.

We learn of the terrorist and CIA connections not from detection but from shifts in the narrative. We know too much that Otani and his men don't know. To make matters worse, no one really learns the identity of Dillon's murderer, although, in a narrative shift, we find that there is someone who does know. This plot strand is simply eclipsed by the espionage element in the story, which itself seems pasted on. The transition from a quiet beginning to a climax of internationally important events is just not smooth.

The story line is disappointing. If the book has anything to recommend it, it is the setting and local color. Melville certainly knows the Japanese milieu. We see Westerners through Otani's eyes and learn cultural tidbits, such as the fact that many Japanese felt shock when, in the late 1950's, they first saw Japanese movie actors and actresses kissing on screen. This sort of thing is interesting in itself, but it would better serve as the background to an interesting plot that is interestingly resolved. (Greg Goode)

Jonathan Valin. *Dead Letter*. Dodd, Mead, 1981, 248 pp., $9.95.

Almost every private eye who debuted in print within the past fifteen years reads like a clone of Ross Macdonald's Lew Archer. He's a man in the midlife-crisis years, full of concern for nature and other people, more at home among families torn by hate than in dark alleys and gangster hangouts, needing to love and be loved infinitely more than to kill and be killed. Jonathan Valin varies the formula by basing his private eye, Harry Stoner, in Cincinnati rather than Southern California and by combining the motifs of Macdonald's Lew Archer novels with the graphic violence of the films of Sam Peckinpah.

In Valin's third novel, an eccentric professor of physics is murdered soon after hiring Stoner to recover quietly an atomic research document which he believes his estranged daughter stole from his safe. The daughter belongs to a club of Marxian environmentalists with a storeroom full of guns and grenades, and Harry is stalked by the unit's psychotic butcher while investigating the academic backstabbings among the dead man's faculty colleagues and trying to fathom the depths of hate between the murdered professor and his strange daughter.

Dead Letter is Valin's most ambitious book to date, a blend of PI detection, brooding over the world, gentle sex, and bloody carnage set among striking characters in a vividly described midwinter Cincinnati. But too many elements of the story seem at least ten years out of date, and the plot is vexed with unnecessary loose ends, vagueness of detail, and

scenes without purpose. Perhaps even worse is that Valin does
almost nothing with the moral ambiguity--Stoner assisting in
what can only be described as official assassination of the
butchering psycho, then breaking relations with the person he
suspects murdered a no-less-sadistic monster a few days earlier
--that lies at the heart of the novel.

It's been five years since the last Lew Archer novel, and
Ross Macdonald's recent stroke may mean that there will be no
more. But with backup Archers like Harry Stoner available,
the aficionado of private-eye literature, though he may not be
totally satisfied, will never despair. (Francis M. Nevins, Jr.)

Gil Brewer. *Angel*. Avon, 1960, 96 pp.

That's right, ninety-six pages, but it seems even shorter.
Brewer is one of those old paperback writers who could keep a
story moving from first page to last. In this one, Nick Gavin
goes back to his Florida hometown in answer to a letter from
an old friend. When he drives up to the friend's house, a man
and woman run out. The friend is inside, dead. There's a gun
on the floor. Guess who picks up the gun just as the police
arrive. Guess who's in big trouble. And it gets worse. The
best friend's wife is one of those Brewer women who is so hot
you could use her to start the fire in your barbecue grill,
and before long old Nick is in the sack with her. And before
long he's hired a detective who gets his throat cut in Nick's
motel room. The only problem with this book is that the reader
figures things out long before Nick does, but then the reader
doesn't have Nick's excuse. Angel--the friend's wife--would
distract anyone. I understand that there's a new movie called
Body Heat and that all the reviewers are recalling James M.
Cain. I have a feeling that it would remind me of Gil Brewer
instead. (Bill Crider)

John Creasey. *The Extortioners*. Scribner's, 1974.

Every time one reads a book by Creasey, the feeling in-
trudes that this is the time when you will find a poor book.
After all, how is it possible to be so prolific and yet turn
out quality at the same time? This book, one in the Roger
"Handsome" West canon, is not that poor book. The book concerns blackmail, motorcycle gangs, and secret business con-
tracts. Somehow Creasey manages to weave all these disparate
elements into a cohesive whole and one that is very believable
at that. No great feats of deduction are performed, but despite that the book leads inevitably to a satisfying conclu-
sion.

In the course of this investigation Roger's life and those
of his family are threatened, and he has to defy his superiors
in New Scotland Yard in order to solve the case. Sergeant
Venables plays a prominent part in the story; several times he
is one step ahead of Roger in his thinking. West's wife and
son also play major roles. (S. Jeffery Koch)

Margaret Truman. *Murder on Capitol Hill*. Arbor House, 1981,
  255 pp., $11.95.

The biggest surprise about Margaret Truman's second pre-packaged, guaranteed-to-make-a-mint mystery is that it's such an improvement over the feeble *Murder in the White House*. Senate Majority Leader Cale Caldwell is stabbed to death with an ice pick during a private party honoring his commitment to federal funding for the arts, and Washington communications lawyer Lydia James, a mature but attractive and dynamic lady with expertise in criminal law and the piano, is hand-picked by the dead man's family-obsessed widow as special counsel to a Senate committee to investigate the murder separately from the police. The crime may be connected with the unsolved murder of Caldwell's adopted daughter two years earlier, or with the religious cult that has ensnared the senator's oldest son, or with the love life of a vicious all-night talk show host, and Lydia uncovers layers of emotional and political intrigue as she reluctantly probes the lives and secrets of her friends.

It's a smoothly written tale, with a neatly sketched background of Washington after hours, some well-choreographed interweavings of suspects and plot threads, and an exception-ally interesting woman protagonist, whose romance with her former music teacher is evoked with exquisite beauty despite the fact that she is forty and he well over sixty. At bottom, however, this is a crime-flavored soap opera, with the police relegated to walk-on parts in the murder investigation and all the whodunit elements kept subordinate at all times to the love entanglements. The truth is finally revealed not by Lydia's detective work but by Truman's having everyone converge on a deserted TV station and blurt out all the book's secrets for no good reason, while a hidden tape recorder just happens to be running. And the cluttered ending is matched by occa-sional silliness over details: Truman ruins her most suspense-ful scene by using the word orthochlorobenzalmalononitrile during a standoff between Lydia and a potential rapist, and she ludicrously conjures up the shades of Sergeant Preston of the Yukon and his faithful dog Yukon King by choosing as the book's final line "This case is closed."

If there is any consistency in life, the third Margaret Truman mystery will be called *Murder at the Supreme Court*. An eminent Justice with scads of ideological and personal enemies will be bludgeoned to death in his chambers with a volume of the Supreme Court Reporter, and the newest member of the Court --a mature but attractive and dynamic lady with expertise in criminal law and the cello?--will be appointed by her col-leagues to investigate the murder separately from the police. The world can hardly wait. (Francis M. Nevins, Jr.)

(Continued from page 41) place where justice is an abstract concept beyond the understanding of her rulers.

The book should not be read and taken seriously as the equivalent of the average American police procedural. There are gaps in the logic as wide as the distance from Leningrad to Novosibirsk. How, for example, could Duvakin possibly pose as a representative of an opposing crime syndicate, shivering away in his threadbare coat and plastic shoes as he does?

Nevertheless, Olcott demonstrates with utmost clarity how it is that a humble man can so easily be caught up out of the problems of his everyday life. That the novel reads as though it were translated directly from the Russian adds an amazing authenticity to the spell-binding chill *(Continued on page 53)*

The Documents In the Case

(Letters)

From Frank Floyd, Rt. 3, Box 139-F, Berryville, AR 72616:
Have you considered doing another Saga? One about Perry
Mason, for instance? Being timid of nature, I would not dare
hint. [*After roughly 115,000 words on Nero Wolfe, I'm about
Sagaed out. But I'd be delighted to run another Saga-type
serial article if someone else'd do all the work.*]

Could you get a message to one of your subscribers and
sometimes contributor, going under the name of Ellen Nehr when
last heard of? Issue after issue, expectantly my vain hope
mounted that Ellen might appear once more in the *FANcier's*
pages; tell her not to worry herself or be concerned about the
harm she has done. Linda Toole is taking her place, or seems
to be, and I certainly am glad someone is. [*I suppose this is
as good a time as any to clear the decks about Ellen Nehr.
Hoaxes can be a lot of fun, but after a while they get old,
and it's best to 'fess up and get on with life. The fact is,
Ellen Nehr is a pen-name that Martin Morse Wooster has been
using in TMF for the past several years. Martin and I both
thought it would be a good joke for him to pen a few letters
and articles under that nom de plume, affecting a style completely at variance with what is normal for him. Frankly, I
sometimes thought that Martin took it a bit too far, writing
some really outrageous stuff which I was certain would tip
everyone off to the fact that Ellen Nehr could not possibly be
a real person. But Martin's judgment appears to have been
better than mine, since to this very day no one has tumbled to
the fact that Ellen Nehr is actually Martin Wooster in drag,
so to speak.*]

Recently I read Johnson's "Rasselas," which reminded me of
something. When I first started reading Nero Wolfe, I thought
that he was drawn from Samuel Johnson. The large bulk, the
quibbling over word usage, the ability to analyze and expound
on complex situations and to compose difficult materials off
the top of his head, his bravery, the dark sulky periods, the
somewhat astringent personality--all are recognizable, in-
grained parts of the day-to-day make-up of both Johnson and
Wolfe.

Another thing I have read recently is Jack Paar's "My
Sword is Bent." Like "Rasselas," this is no mystery, but it
is still worthwhile, to my mind, and I found a particularly
interesting tidbit on page xvii. "During the sixty years between 1895 and 1955, the fifteen best sellers in this country

included nine novels, three inspirational books, two cookbooks and one baby book. Of the nine novels that made the best seller list, seven were by Mickey Spillane." Of course, I cannot say if it is true, nor have I any idea where Paar got his information.

I just re-read thirty or forty of Steve Lewis's book reviews. They are still as absorbing as the first time (my test for value and excellence, which almost nothing passes; probably not more than two percent). Strangely, virtually all the rest of the *FANcier* is good reading the second time around, too. Looking over the covers, my favorite was the news article concerning the wealthy editor whose death is assumed to have been caused by terminal embarrassment. Townsend, I think his name was.

From Linda Toole, 40 Hermitage Rd., Rochester, NY 14617:

I guess we'll have to accept your word on the Stout bibliography, although the four of you may have made a gigantic error by including articles for the Wolfe Pack's *Gazette*, numbers three and four. At the rate they are being published (none since March, 1980), the bibliography may just be the only place they ever see print! [*Yes, those* Gazette *articles are becoming something of an embarrassment. In fact, I have it on good authority that the type for all the articles has been set--for years now, it seems--but that the powers that be in the Wolfe Pack have yet to get off their duffs and have the issues printed. This past summer I offered to take over the publication, but no one even bothered to respond. Hell, I've been trying for two years now just to subscribe to the* Gazette, *but I can't even find anyone who will take my money. It's a hell of a way to run a railroad.*]

My thanks to Steve Stilwell for his recommendation of the Heritage Press edition of *Drood*. So far I've been unable to locate a copy, so if anyone out there knows of one for sale . . . . Rhetorical question--Why do people always recommend books that are out of print?

Bob Napier's thoughts on the TV Nero Wolfe were appreciated. We are in agreement on many points, although I can't help feeling that his viewpoint was rather jaundiced. The article gave me the impression that he expected a failure because it was television. I do agree that several TV movies would probably have been the best way to go. I recently had the pleasure of seeing (again) the TV pilot of *The Doorbell Rang* (1970) with Thayer David as Wolfe. We lost a good Wolfe when David died. Perhaps the best casting was Cramer, however. Biff McGuire may not have fit my physical idea of Cramer, but he *felt* right. Horsley is Archie. (Of course, I've never met Guy or Bill Crider, but so far he fits.)

This summer I had the pleasure of meeting and talking with David and Dorothy Doerrer. And just recently I had the pleasure of visiting John and Ruth McAleer and seeing his collection of Stout and other mysteries--impressive is an understatement. We spent almost three hours with John and the collection and could have spent as many days. It's always enjoyable to meet fellow fans, so if any of you happen to visit Rochester and have a few extra minutes, please give me a call (hey-- it *could* happen!).

From Greg Goode, 50 Washburn Park, Rochester, NY 14620:

I am a new subscriber to TMF; I've seen about six issues, and I feel as addicted as the old timers. [. . .]

A few issues back, Al Hubin mentioned that he'd try to do an update on the *Bibliography*, including a locations index. I'm all for that, and I might as well sign up right now to purchase a copy.

And I agree with Bill Crider, who said in 5:5 that Walter Albert ought to do a film column, even if he has to be bribed. I think that this season will offer plenty of mysterious movies: *True Confessions* (crime, at least), *I, The Jury*, *Looker*, *Rollover*, and a few others I can't recall right now. And if there's a dry spell, he can do retros, and we can all look forward to *Hammett* . . . . [*Walter, your public calls.*]

From Walter & Jean Shine, 122 Lakeshore Dr., N. Palm Beach, FL:

Away for the summer, several issues of TMF appeared in the accumulation of bills, catalogs, bills, charitable organization requests for contributions, bills, and a $14 tax refund from the IRS. Yes, GMT, there is a reward for good guys, too.

Thanks for the mention of our *John D. MacDonald Bibliography*, even though you deplored the lack of a review copy. 'Tis the U. of Florida which handles distribution of copies (and receives all proceeds--our labor was one of love, not profit), and we will ask them on your behalf. But, after reading Walter Albert's brilliant review (in TMF 5:3, pp. 5-10) of the Skene Melvin work, we're not sure we want to be subjected to so painstaking an analysis. . . . Nonetheless, if a copy of our work comes to your attention (or to Albert's), do remember that, though novices in the bibliographic art, we did try, as he says the bibliographer must, "to make information available in as economical, straightforward, and [as] accurate [a] manner as possible." We would welcome your (or his) verdict. [. . .]

Robert Samoian (TMF 5:4, pp. 40-41) writes of publishers' errors with respect to authors' names. Here's a twist on the theme (brought to our attention by Steve Scott of Rockville, Maryland) in a Crest paperback published in March 1960, entitled *The Chased and the Unchaste* by (you have our oath on this!) Thomas B. Dewey. Fair enough, except the last page ends as follows:

THE END
of a Crest reprint by
John D. MacDonald

Crest, an arm of Fawcett Books, has, along with Fawcett, done considerable violence to some of the JDM books, all of which you may read eventually when they appear in our forthcoming *Potpourri of Printings: The Books of John D. MacDonald*, in which we will try to give identifying details of every printing of every JDM book.

[*From a later letter:*] Back from a week's trip (two days of which at the JDM collection at the University of Florida in Gainesville, updating our *JDM Bibliography* with info from nine boxes of materials he had sent since the spring of this year) to find the batch of old--but good!--back issues you'd sent.

Several comments: your zine is outstanding, and is obviously a back-breaking job. Why not simplify your life a bit and have a standard format for contributions so that you do not have to re-type them except in rare instances? We submit out "Shine Section" to the *JDM Bibliophile* picture-ready so that nothing has to be done by the editor (except read it--which we sometimes doubt he does). Scissors and paste would make your life relatively simple and would enable you to avoid re-typing if this suggestion were adopted--and, to anticipate, nobody would object to different typewriter faces; au contraire, they might have additional reader attraction. [*You are quite right that I could save great amounts of time by simply scissor-and-pasting up each issue from the manuscripts as they are submitted, but the result would look like a scissor-and-paste job, and I'm inclined to think it would have more reader repulsion than reader attraction. The only thing I print as submitted is Dave Doerrer's annual index of books reviewed in TMF. I hate typing lists so much that I'd probably shoot it directly from his pages even if David didn't do his accustomed, neat job of typing it up.*]

Even if you don't do that, why not cut down a bit on those comments such as "Enjoyed the latest issue of *The Mystery FANcier* as usual"; if they didn't, they probably wouldn't take pen in hand. Having said that, we also realize you've cut down considerably in the latest issues on that habit, so perhaps this comment is out-of-date. Even so, *we* find TMF filled with all kinds of information previously unknown to us--although there is a dearth of JDM comment--but after all, anything with periodic comments and reviews by Mike Nevins can't be all bad!

A footnote to our mention in our last letter to you: included in our forthcoming *Potpourri of Printings* will be complete listings of all JDM's cover illustrators, thus gladdening Art Scott's heart and helping him complete the checklist of the covers and paintings by the great Robert McGinnis.

'Nuff for now, Squinty, we'll see you at Bouchercon in Milwaukee (our first); look for that gorgeous, tall, thin, sexy blonde and her goggle-eyed, bulging, gray-haired, sexagenarian escort. [. . .]

P.S. Learned that Walter Albert bought *two* copies of our *JDM Bibliography*. Perhaps he'll review it for your TMF? [*How about it, Walter.*]

From Charles Shibuk, 2084 Bronx Park East, Bronx, NY 10462:
Bob Napier's article on the Nero Wolfe TV series is a thoughtful effort to point out its flaws and strengths and evaluate the reasons for its ultimate failure. I watched the first entry in the series and was discouraged from watching any later episodes. However, that entry seems a masterpiece and a model of screen adaptation when compared to the legendary (but awful) 1936 film, *Meet Nero Wolfe*, which recently, for the first time in many decades, had a very brief screening in an out-of-the-way N.Y.C. revival house--and even that was more than it deserved!

Meet Nero Wolfe is based on *Fer-de-Lance* and stars Edward Arnold in the title role. Arnold was an extremely fine (and underrated) actor and is perhaps an even better choice than Orson Welles for the role. Unfortunately, he is misdirected into smiling, chuckling, or laughing at everything during the course of the film.

Lionel Stander is wildly miscast as Archie and does little more than contribute his magnificently rasping voice to the proceedings.

As far as fidelity to the characters goes (this film was

released in 1936, remember), *Meet Nero Wolfe* starts with Wolfe opening the door to Archie and his fiancée. The film ends with the couple, now happily married, leaving the house, while the blushing bride is soundly kissed goodbye by Wolfe.

There are a couple of scenes showing Wolfe opening beer bottles and depositing their caps in an already overloaded desk drawer, but I don't think the fictional Wolfe ever drank straight from the bottle.

Culinary purists in this area will certainly be offended by the scene where Archie and his lady-love arrive late for a meal and are served hot dogs as an extreme form of punishment. Rex Stout, needless to say, was not amused.

The TV mentality can be criticized for the flaws in the recent series, but it would seem that Hollywood had much more to answer for.

From Bill Crider, 4206 Ninth Street, Brownwood, TX 76801:
My typer seems to have had a mind of its own last time I wrote, so now I'll try and correct its errors. Of course I meant to refer to Augustus Mandrell and to Dexter St. Clair, not to Agustus Mandress and Dester St. Clair. (You'll notice I'm carefully accepting the blame and not accusing you of errors; I still don't want that story about the WAFs and the Ovaltine to get out. [*That's certainly the wisest course.*])

From Bob Adey, 7 Highcroft Avenue, Wordsley, Stourbridge, West Midlands, DY8 5LX, England:
This letter is occasioned by the recent arrival of your flyer for Brownstone Books and the September/October 1981 TMF. This particular issue of TMF had, incidentally, all the classic hallmarks--the enlightened articles, the thoughtful reviews, the punchy letters, the change of address. Yes, everything that has made TMF what it is today! [. . .]

A nice batch of reviews in this issue of TMF. Steve Lewis is someone I can usually rely upon to like the same sort of book I do, but we differ completely on Robert B. Gillespie's *Crossword Mystery*. I found it unusual, well written, cleverly constructed, and with the crossword element (which can be so tiresome) unobtrusively, yet interestingly used.

Martin Wooster requests reviews of British TV mysteries. One word will do for the recent three-part serialisation of Donald Gordon's *Rose Medallion*--awful. A pity, too, as it featured that rara avis, the British private eye. The two Martin particularly mentioned, Sapphire and Steel and The Professionals, I'll deal with as a separate item. And I'll try to let you have more as they occur to me--or as I'm asked for them. [*Consider yourself asked.*]

From Mary Seeger, 6977 Alaska Ave. S.E., Caledonia, MI 49316:
Can you suggest where I might buy a set of the Nicaraguan "famous detectives" stamps? (Mine have disappeared, probably in a book.) [*Can anyone help Mary with this?*]

(Continued from page 48) of the story itself.
The ending is not easily forgotten. It is a manufactured one, true, but it is also one which reverberates in the reader's memory for a long time afterwards, like the distant clang of a door in a far-off Siberian jail cell. (B minus)*

U.S. POSTAL SERVICE

STATEMENT OF OWNERSHIP, MANAGEMENT AND CIRCULATION
(Required by 39 U.S.C. 3685)

1. TITLE OF PUBLICATION	A. PUBLICATION NO.	2. DATE OF FILING
The Mystery Fancier	4 2 8 5 9 0	29 September 1981

3. FREQUENCY OF ISSUE	A. NO. OF ISSUES PUBLISHED ANNUALLY	B. ANNUAL SUBSCRIPTION PRICE
Bi-monthly	6	$12.00

4. COMPLETE MAILING ADDRESS OF KNOWN OFFICE OF PUBLICATION *(Street, City, County, State and ZIP Code) (Not printers)*

Guy M. Townsend, 1711 Clifty Dr., Madison, IN 47250 (Jefferson County)

5. COMPLETE MAILING ADDRESS OF THE HEADQUARTERS OR GENERAL BUSINESS OFFICES OF THE PUBLISHERS *(Not printers)*

Same

6. FULL NAMES AND COMPLETE MAILING ADDRESS OF PUBLISHER, EDITOR, AND MANAGING EDITOR *(This item MUST NOT be blank)*

PUBLISHER *(Name and Complete Mailing Address)*

Same

EDITOR *(Name and Complete Mailing Address)*

Same

MANAGING EDITOR *(Name and Complete Mailing Address)*

Same

7. OWNER *(If owned by a corporation, its name and address must be stated and also immediately thereunder the names and addresses of stockholders owning or holding 1 percent or more of total amount of stock. If not owned by a corporation, the names and addresses of the individual owners must be given. If owned by a partnership or other unincorporated firm, its name and address, as well as that of each individual must be given. If the publication is published by a nonprofit organization, its name and address must be stated.) (Item must be completed)*

FULL NAME	COMPLETE MAILING ADDRESS
Guy M. Townsend (sole owner)	1711 Clifty Dr., Madison, IN 47250

8. KNOWN BONDHOLDERS, MORTGAGEES, AND OTHER SECURITY HOLDERS OWNING OR HOLDING 1 PERCENT OR MORE OF TOTAL AMOUNT OF BONDS, MORTGAGES OR OTHER SECURITIES *(If there are none, so state)*

FULL NAME	COMPLETE MAILING ADDRESS
None	

9. FOR COMPLETION BY NONPROFIT ORGANIZATIONS AUTHORIZED TO MAIL AT SPECIAL RATES *(Section 411.3, DMM only)*
The purpose, function, and nonprofit status of this organization and the exempt status for Federal income tax purposes *(Check one)*

(1) ☐ HAS NOT CHANGED DURING PRECEDING 12 MONTHS	(2) ☐ HAS CHANGED DURING PRECEDING 12 MONTHS	*(If changed, publisher must submit explanation of change with this statement.)*

10. EXTENT AND NATURE OF CIRCULATION	AVERAGE NO. COPIES EACH ISSUE DURING PRECEDING 12 MONTHS	ACTUAL NO. COPIES OF SINGLE ISSUE PUBLISHED NEAREST TO FILING DATE
A. TOTAL NO. COPIES *(Net Press Run)*	250	250
B. PAID CIRCULATION 1. SALES THROUGH DEALERS AND CARRIERS, STREET VENDORS AND COUNTER SALES	17	22
2. MAIL SUBSCRIPTION	197	191
C. TOTAL PAID CIRCULATION *(Sum of 10B1 and 10B2)*	214	213
D. FREE DISTRIBUTION BY MAIL, CARRIER OR OTHER MEANS SAMPLES, COMPLIMENTARY, AND OTHER FREE COPIES	10	12
E. TOTAL DISTRIBUTION *(Sum of C and D)*	224	225
F. COPIES NOT DISTRIBUTED 1. OFFICE USE, LEFT OVER, UNACCOUNTED, SPOILED AFTER PRINTING	26	25
2. RETURN FROM NEWS AGENTS	0	0
G. TOTAL *(Sum of E, F1 and 2 - should equal net press run shown in A)*	250	250

11. I certify that the statements made by me above are correct and complete	SIGNATURE AND TITLE OF EDITOR, PUBLISHER, BUSINESS MANAGER, OR OWNER *[signature]* Editor

PS Form
June 1980 3526 (Page 1)   *(See Instruction on reverse)*

www.ingramcontent.com/pod-product-compliance
Lightning Source LLC
Chambersburg PA
CBHW031614040426

42452CB00006B/525